Spanish for Health Professionals

INTERACTIVE LANGUAGE EXERCISES

Doctors, Dentists, Nurses, Psychologists,
Social Workers & Related Fields

■

Inglés para Profesionistas de la Salud

EJERCICIOS INTERACTIVOS DE LENGUAJE

Doctores, Dentistas, Enfermeras, Sicólogos,
Trabajadores Sociales y campos afines

Darío Sánchez

Rubén Juárez

Computer
Resources
Associates, Inc.

Significant Learning Series
Serie Aprendizaje Significativo

Title: *Spanish for Health Professionals / Inglés para Profesionistas de la Salud*

Book, CD/Audio, CD/Multimedia and cassette.

Significant Learning Series. CRA Inc.

System requirements: CD-ROM, Windows 95 or Windows NT®

All inquiries should be addressed to:

CRA Inc.

e-mail: SpanishBooks@CRA-USA.com

First printed in July 1997

Printed in the United States of America

ISBN N° 0-9658803-1-1Spanish for Health Professionals.

Index / Índice

At the Receptionist / Con la recepcionista

1

Recepcionista:	Buenos días.
Cliente:	Buenos días señorita. Tengo cita con el (la) doctor(a) a las nueve.
Receptionist:	Good morning.
Client:	Good morning. I have an appointment with the doctor at nine.

2

Recepcionista:	Buenas tardes.
Cliente:	Buenas tardes señorita. Quisiera ver al (a la) doctor(a).
Receptionist:	Good afternoon.
Client:	Good afternoon. I would like to see the doctor.

3

Recepcionista:	¿Tiene cita hoy?
Cliente:	Sí, a las ocho y media.
Receptionist:	Do you have an appointment today?
Client:	Yes, at eight thirty.

4

Recepcionista:	¿A qué hora?
Cliente:	A las cuatro de la tarde.
Receptionist:	At what time?
Client:	At four p.m.

5

Recepcionista:	¿Con qué doctor?
Cliente:	Con el (la) doctor(a) Schwartz.
Receptionist:	With which doctor?
Client:	With Doctor Schwartz.

6

Recepcionista:	¿Trae su seguro médico?
Cliente:	Sí, aquí está.
Receptionist:	Did you bring your medical insurance?
Client:	Yes, here it is.

7

Recepcionista:	El (La) doctor(a) lo (la) verá en un momento.
Cliente:	Muchas gracias.
Receptionist:	The doctor will see you in a minute.
Client:	Thank you very much.

8

Recepcionista:	En un momento lo (la) atendemos.
Cliente:	Gracias, aquí espero.
Receptionist:	We will see you in a minute.
Client:	Thank you, I will wait here.

9

Recepcionista:	Espere aquí por favor.
Cliente:	Gracias.
Receptionist:	Wait here please.
Client:	Thank you.

10

Recepcionista:	Tome asiento por favor.
Cliente:	Muchas gracias.
Receptionist:	Have a seat, please.
Client:	Thank you.

11

Recepcionista:	Sígame por aquí, por favor.
Cliente:	Un momento, voy a tomar mis cosas.
Receptionist:	This way please.
Client:	Just a minute, I'm going to get my things.

12

Recepcionista:	Va a tener que esperar un momento, por favor.
Cliente:	Espero que no tarde mucho.
Receptionist:	You are going to have to wait for a minute.
Client:	I hope it won't take too long.

13

Recepcionista:	El (La) doctor(a) todavía no llega.
Cliente:	¿A qué hora lo (la) esperan?
Receptionist:	The doctor has not arrived.
Client:	When do you expect him (her)?

14

Recepcionista: El (La) doctor(a) va a llegar tarde.
Cliente: Prefiero cambiar mi cita para otro día.
Receptionist: The doctor is going to be late.
Client: I would rather change my appointment for another day.

15

Recepcionista: Su cita se ha cancelado.
Cliente: ¿Pero por qué?
Receptionist: Your appointment has been canceled.
Client: But why?

16

Recepcionista: ¿Quiere hacer otra cita?
Cliente: Sí, para el martes si es posible.
Receptionist: Do you want to make another appointment?
Client: Yes, for next Tuesday if possible.

17

Cliente: ¿Dónde está el baño?
Recepcionista: El baño está a la derecha.
Client: Where is the bathroom?
Receptionist: The bathroom is to your right.

18

Cliente: ¿Dónde está la farmacia?
Recepcionista: La farmacia está a la izquierda.
Client: Where is the pharmacy?
Receptionist: The pharmacy is to your left.

19

Cliente:	¿Dónde está el laboratorio?
Recepcionista:	El laboratorio está al final del pasillo.
Client:	Where is the laboratory?
Receptionist:	The laboratory is at the end of the hall.

20

Recepcionista:	¿Trae sus papeles?
Cliente:	Sí, aquí están.
Receptionist:	Did you bring your papers?
Client:	Yes, here they are.

21

Recepcionista:	Espere a que le llamen por favor.
Cliente:	¿Tardará mucho?
Receptionist:	Wait until you are called, please.
Client:	Will it take long?

22

Recepcionista:	Llene esta forma por favor.
Cliente:	Esa forma ya la llené.
Receptionist:	Fill out this form, please.
Client:	I have already filled out this form.

23

Recepcionista:	¿Necesita un lápiz?
Cliente:	No, gracias.
Receptionist:	Do you need a pencil?
Client:	No. Thank you

24

Recepcionista:	Firme aquí.
Cliente:	¿Para qué es este documento?
Receptionist:	Sign here please.
Client:	What is this document for?

25

Recepcionista:	Pase a recoger sus medicinas a la farmacia.
Cliente:	¿Dónde queda la farmacia?
Receptionist:	Pick up your medications at the pharmacy.
Client:	Where is the pharmacy?

Answering the Phone
Contestando el teléfono

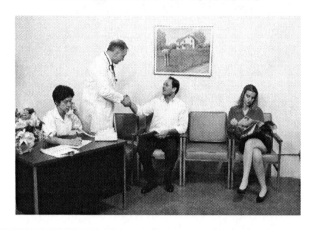

26

Recepcionista: ¿Bueno?
Cliente: ¿Se encuentra el (la) doctor(a)?
Receptionist: Hello?
Client: Is the doctor in?

27

Recepcionista: ¿Cuál es su nombre?
Cliente: Antonio Pérez.
Receptionist: Your name please?
Client: Antonio Perez.

28

Recepcionista: ¿Con quién quiere hablar?
Cliente: Con el (la) doctor(a) Schwartz.
Receptionist: Who do you want to talk to?
Client: With doctor Shwartz.

29

Recepcionista: Un momento, por favor no cuelgue.
Cliente: Sí, espero.
Receptionist: One minute, please don't hang up.
Client: OK, I'll wait.

30

Recepcionista: Voy a transferir su llamada, no cuelgue.
Cliente: Gracias.
Receptionist: I'm going to transfer your call, don't hang up.
Client: Thank you.

31

Recepcionista: El (La) doctor(a) está ocupado(a).
Cliente: ¿A qué hora debo hablarle?
Receptionist: The Doctor is busy.
Client: At what time should I call him (her) back?

32

Recepcionista: ¿Quiere dejar su nombre y número de teléfono?
Cliente: Mi nombre es Rodrigo Villaseñor y mi teléfono es 135-7980
Receptionist: Would you like to leave your name and phone number?
Client: My name is Rodrigo Villaseñor and my phone number is 135-7980.

33

Recepcionista: El (La) doctor(a) no está, regresa por la tarde.
Cliente: Bien, le llamaré más tarde.
Receptionist: The Doctor is not in, he (she) will be back this afternoon.
Client: Fine, I will call him (her) later.

34

Recepcionista:	El (La) doctor(a) no está, regresa la semana próxima.
Cliente:	¿Puedo hacer una cita para cuando regrese?
Receptionist:	The Doctor is not in, he (she) will be back next week.
Client:	Can I make an appointment for when he(she) gets back?

35

Recepcionista:	El (La) doctor(a) regresa en 10 minutos.
Cliente:	Vuelvo a llamar más tarde.
Receptionist:	The Doctor will be back in 10 minutes.
Client:	I will call later.

36

Recepcionista:	El (La) doctor(a) regresa hasta mañana.
Cliente:	¿Puedo dejarle un mensaje?
Receptionist:	The Doctor will be back tomorrow.
Client:	Can I leave a message?

37

Recepcionista:	Esa persona ya no trabaja aquí.
Cliente:	¿Puede decirme dónde trabaja?
Receptionist:	This person no longer works here.
Client:	Can you tell me where he (she) works now?

38

Recepcionista:	El (La) doctor(a) está de vacaciones.
Cliente:	¿Cuándo regresa?
Receptionist:	The Doctor is out on vacation.
Client:	When will he (she) be back?

39

Recepcionista: El (La) doctor(a) está con un paciente.

Cliente: ¿A qué hora se desocupa?

Receptionist: The Doctor is with a patient.

Client: At what time will he (she) be available?

40

Recepcionista: ¿Quiere hacer una cita con el (la) doctor(a)?

Cliente: Sí, ¿será posible a las cuatro de la tarde?

Receptionist: Do you want to make an appointment with the doctor?

Client: Yes, would it be possible at four in the afternoon?

41

Recepcionista: ¿Quiere una cita de urgencia?

Cliente: Sí, tengo un dolor muy fuerte.

Receptionist: Do you need an urgent appointment?

Client: Yes, I have a very severe pain.

42

Recepcionista: ¿Con cuál doctor quiere hacer una cita?

Cliente: Con el (la) doctor(a) Martínez.

Receptionist: With which doctor do you want to make an appointment?

Client: With Doctor Martinez.

43

Recepcionista: Por las mañanas el (la) doctor(a) está muy ocupado.

Cliente: ¿Qué día puede recibirme por la mañana?

Receptionist: The Doctor is very busy in the mornings.

Client: What day can he (she) see me in the morning?

44

Recepcionista:	¿Qué día es mejor para usted?
Cliente:	El martes por la tarde.
Receptionist:	What day is good for you?
Client:	Tuesday afternoon.

45

Recepcionista:	¿A qué hora prefiere que le hagamos su cita?
Cliente:	Lo más pronto posible. Es urgente.
Receptionist:	At what time would you like to make your appointment?
Client:	As soon as possible. This is urgent.

46

Recepcionista:	¿Es una emergencia?
Cliente:	No, sólo quiero hacer una pregunta.
Receptionist:	Is this an emergency?
Client:	No, I just want to ask a question.

47

Recepcionista:	¿Quiere cancelar su cita?
Cliente:	Sí, no puedo ir esta tarde.
Receptionist:	Do you want to cancel your appointment?
Client:	Yes, I can't make it this afternoon.

48

Recepcionista:	¿Quiere cambiar su cita?
Cliente:	Sí, para el próximo jueves por favor.
Receptionist:	Do you want to change your appointment?
Client:	Yes, to next Thursday please.

49

Recepcionista: ¿Me permite su número de seguro médico?

Cliente: Sí, mi número es 246-357-089-1.

Receptionist: Can I have your medical insurance number?

Client: Yes my number is 246-357-089-1.

50

Recepcionista: Traiga todas las medicinas que está tomando.

Cliente: ¿Incluyendo las que me recetó el (la) siquiatra?

Receptionist: Bring all the medications that you are taking.

Client: Including the ones prescribed by the psychiatrist?

CHAPTER 3 / CAPÍTULO 3

Vital Signs / Signos vitales

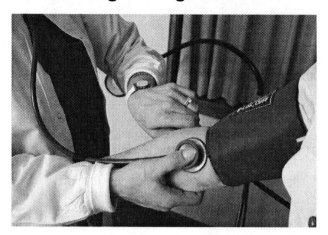

51

Enfermera:	Siéntese aquí por favor.
Cliente:	Gracias.
Nurse:	Have a seat here please.
Client:	Thank you.

52

Enfermera:	Abra la boca.
Cliente:	Sí.
Nurse:	Open your mouth.
Client:	O.K.

53

Enfermera:	Le voy a tomar la temperatura.
Cliente:	¿Tengo fiebre?
Nurse:	I'm going to take your temperature.
Client:	Do I have a fever?

54

Enfermera:	Le voy a tomar el pulso.
Cliente:	¿Es normal mi pulso?
Nurse:	I'm going to take your pulse.
Client:	Is my pulse normal?

55

Enfermera:	Le voy a tomar la presión.
Cliente:	¿Cuál es mi presión?
Nurse:	I'm going to take your blood pressure.
Client:	What is my blood pressure?

56

Enfermera:	Súbase aquí para pesarlo(a).
Cliente:	¿Cuánto peso?
Nurse:	Step up here so I can weigh you.
Client:	How much do I weigh?

CHAPTER 4 / CAPÍTULO 4

The Interview / La entrevista

57

Trabajador social:	¿Cómo ha estado? Le voy a hacer unas preguntas.
Cliente:	Está bien.
Social Worker:	How are you doing? I'm going to ask you some questions.
Client:	Fine.

58

Trabajador social:	¿Cómo se llama?
Cliente:	Roberto Miramontes.
Social Worker:	What is your name?
Client:	Roberto Miramontes.

59

Trabajador social:	¿Cuál es su dirección?
Cliente:	25789 Vía de la Plaza.
Social Worker:	What is your address?
Client:	25789 Vía de la Plaza.

60

Trabajador social: ¿Número y calle donde vive?
Cliente: 1390 Caminito Cerrado.
Social Worker: Number and street where you live?
Client: 1390 Caminito Cerrado.

61

Trabajador social: ¿Cuál es su código postal?
Cliente: No lo sé, me acabo de cambiar.
Social Worker: What is your zip code?
Client: I don't know, I just moved.

62

Trabajador social: ¿Cuánto tiempo tiene viviendo aquí?
Cliente: Cuatro años.
Social Worker: How long have you lived here?
Client: Four years.

63

Trabajador social: ¿Cuál es su número de teléfono?
Cliente: Área 246, número 3574680.
Social Worker: What is your phone number?
Client: Area code 246, number 3574680.

64

Trabajador social: ¿Cuál es su fecha de nacimiento?
Cliente: Julio 12 de 1968.
Social Worker: Your date of birth?
Client: July 12, 1968.

65

Trabajador social:	¿Cuántos años tiene?
Cliente:	55 años de edad.
Social Worker:	How old are you?
Client:	55 years old.

66

Trabajador social:	¿En dónde nació?
Cliente:	En México.
Social Worker:	Where were you born?
Client:	In Mexico.

67

Trabajador social:	¿A qué grupo étnico pertenece?
Cliente:	Hispano.
Social Worker:	To which ethnic group do you belong?
Client:	Hispanic.

68

Trabajador social:	¿Cuál es su altura?
Cliente:	Seis pies con tres pulgadas.
Social Worker:	How tall are you?
Client:	Six feet and three inches.

69

Trabajador social:	¿Cuánto pesa?
Cliente:	Ciento cincuenta libras.
Social Worker:	How much do you weight?
Client:	One Hundred and fifty pounds.

70

Trabajador social:	¿De qué color son sus ojos?
Cliente:	Azules.
Social Worker:	What color are your eyes?
Client:	Blue.

71

Trabajador social:	¿De qué color es su cabello?
Cliente:	Negro.
Social Worker:	What color is your hair?
Client:	Black.

72

Trabajador social:	¿Tiene algunas cicatrices?
Cliente:	Sí, en la espalda.
Social Worker:	Do you have any scars?
Client:	Yes, on my back.

73

Trabajador social:	¿Tiene seguro médico?
Cliente:	No, voy a pagar con mi dinero.
Social Worker:	Do you have medical insurance?
Client:	No, I'm paying out of my own pocket.

74

Trabajador social:	¿Tiene MediCal?
Cliente:	Sí, pero no tengo la tarjeta.
Social Worker:	Do you have MediCal?
Client:	Yes, but I don't have the card.

75

Trabajador social:	¿Tiene Medicare?
Cliente:	No, pero lo voy a tramitar.
Social Worker:	Do you have Medicare?
Client:	No, but I'm going to apply for it.

76

Trabajador social:	¿Hasta qué grado escolar cursó?
Cliente:	Hasta preparatoria.
Social Worker:	Up to what grade did you attend in school?
Client:	Up to high school.

77

Trabajador social:	¿Cuál es su estado civil?
Cliente:	Casado(a), Soltero(a), Divorciado(a), Viudo(a), Separado(a), Unión libre.
Social Worker:	What is your marital status?
Client:	Married, Single, Divorced, Widower, Separated, Living together.

78

Trabajador social:	¿Cómo se llama su esposa(o)?
Cliente:	Teresa Mandujano.
Social Worker:	What is your wife's name?
Client:	Teresa Mandujano.

79

Trabajador social:	¿Cómo se llama su esposo(a)?
Cliente:	Rodrigo Mandujano.
Social Worker:	What is your husband's name?
Client:	Rodrigo Mandujano.

80

Trabajador social:	¿Cuál es su religión?
Cliente:	Católica.
Social Worker:	What is your religion?
Client:	Catholic.

81

Trabajador social:	¿En caso de emergencia con quién debemos comunicarnos?
Cliente:	Con mi tía Martha.
Social Worker:	In case of emergency, whom should we contact?
Client:	My aunt Martha.

82

Trabajador social:	¿En dónde vive su familiar más cercano?
Cliente:	En San Francisco, mi hermano Pedro Sandoval.
Social Worker:	Where does your nearest relative live?
Client:	In San Francisco, my brother Pedro Sandoval.

83

Trabajador social:	¿Qué relación tiene esta persona con usted?
Cliente:	Es mi vecina(o).
Social Worker:	How is this person related to you?
Client:	She (He) is my neighbor.

84

Trabajador social:	¿Tiene licencia de manejar?
Cliente:	Sí, pero se me perdió.
Social Worker:	Do you have a driver's license?
Client:	Yes, but I lost it.

85

Trabajador social:	¿Cuál es el número de su licencia de manejar?
Cliente:	A235689
Social Worker:	What's your driver's license number?
Client:	A235689

86

Trabajador social:	¿Dónde trabaja?
Cliente:	En el supermercado.
Social Worker:	Where do you work?
Client:	At the supermarket.

87

Trabajador social:	¿Dónde y cuándo fue la última vez que trabajó?
Cliente:	Hace un año, en el campo.
Social Worker:	Where and when was the last time you worked?
Client:	A year ago in the fields.

88

Trabajador social:	¿Cuántos años ha trabajado en este lugar?
Cliente:	2 años aproximadamente.
Social Worker:	How many years have you worked there?
Client:	Approximately 2 years.

89

Trabajador social:	¿Cuál es el número de teléfono de su trabajo?
Cliente:	2342346, extensión 709.
Social Worker:	What is your phone number at work?
Client:	234-2346, extension 709.

90

Trabajador social:	¿Cuáles son los ingresos mensuales de su familia?
Cliente:	Mil quinientos dólares, más o menos.
Social Worker:	What's your family's monthly income?
Client:	Fifteen hundred dollars, more or less.

91

Trabajador social:	¿Recibe usted beneficios del seguro social?
Cliente:	Todavía no, mis papeles están en trámite.
Social Worker:	Do you get any Social Security benefits?
Client:	Not yet, my documents are being processed.

92

Trabajador social:	¿Cuáles son sus ingresos de SSI?
Cliente:	$450 al mes.
Social Worker:	What is your income from SSI?
Client:	$450 monthly.

93

Trabajador social:	¿Cuánto recibe de SSA?
Cliente:	Creo que son $387 al mes.
Social Worker:	How much do you get from SSA?
Client:	I believe it's $387 a month.

94

Trabajador social:	¿Recibe dinero por concepto de AFDC?
Cliente:	Solamente $207.
Social Worker:	Do you receive AFDC moneys?
Client:	Only $207.

95

Trabajador social:	¿Cuánto recibe de VA?
Cliente:	$987, desde el año pasado.
Social Worker:	How much do you get from VA?
Client:	$987 since last year.

96

Trabajador social:	¿Recibe cupones de comida?
Cliente:	Sí, pero se van a suspender pronto.
Social Worker:	Do you get food stamps?
Client:	Yes, but they will soon be suspended.

97

Trabajador social:	¿Cuánto recibe de Sección 8?
Cliente:	$234, pero espero un incremento.
Social Worker:	How much do you get from Section 8?
Client:	$234, but I'm expecting an increase.

98

Trabajador social:	¿Recibe ingresos de cualquier otra fuente?
Cliente:	No tengo más ingresos.
Social Worker:	Do you receive income from any other source?
Client:	I have no other income.

99

Trabajador social:	¿Quién lo refirió con nosotros?
Cliente:	El (La) doctor(a) Smith.
Social Worker:	Who referred you to us?
Client:	Doctor Smith.

Trabajador social:	¿Qué agencia lo (la) mandó aquí?
Cliente:	El Departamento de Salud.
Social Worker:	What agency sent you here?
Client:	The Department of Health.

During an Emergency
Durante una emergencia

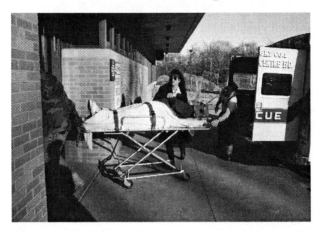

101

Doctor: ¿Tiene dolor en el pecho?

Cliente: No, pero me duele la cabeza.

Doctor: Do you have chest pain?

Client: No, but my head hurts.

102

Doctor: ¿Está sudando?

Cliente: Un poco.

Doctor: Are you sweating?

Client: A bit.

103

Doctor: ¿Tiene dificultad para respirar?

Cliente: Sí, siento como que me estoy asfixiando.

Doctor: Do you have any difficulty breathing?

Client: Yes, I feel like I'm choking.

104

Doctor: ¿Le duele el brazo?

Cliente: Sí, me duele el brazo izquierdo.

Doctor: Does your arm hurt?

Client: Yes, my left arm hurts.

105

Doctor: ¿Le duele el cuello?

Cliente: Mucho, me duele cuando muevo la cabeza

Doctor: Does your neck hurt?

Client: A lot, it hurts when I move my head.

106

Doctor: ¿Le duele la mandíbula?

Cliente: Sí, me duele mucho.

Doctor: Does your jaw hurt?

Client: Yes, it hurts a lot.

107

Doctor: ¿Le duele la quijada?

Cliente: Todo el tiempo.

Doctor: Does your jaw hurt?

Client: All the time.

108

Doctor: ¿Tiene náusea?

Cliente: Sí, siento ganas de vomitar.

Doctor: Do you feel nauseated?

Client: Yes, I feel like vomiting.

109

Doctor: ¿Se siente mareada(o)?
Cliente: Sí, me siento mal. Siento que todo me da vueltas.
Doctor: Do you feel dizzy?
Client: Yes, I feel sick. I feel my head spinning.

110

Doctor: ¿Tiene el pulso rápido o irregular?
Cliente: No sé. Me siento mareada(o).
Doctor: Is your pulse fast or irregular?
Client: I don't know, I feel dizzy.

111

Doctor: ¿Está alguien más con usted?
Cliente: Sí, mi tío(a).
Doctor: Are you with someone else?
Client: Yes, with my uncle (aunt).

112

Doctor: Quiero hablar con otra persona.
Cliente: Estoy sola(o).
Doctor: I would like to speak with someone else.
Client: I'm alone.

113

Doctor: ¿Le han diagnosticado alguna enfermedad del corazón?
Cliente: Sí, angina de pecho.
Doctor: Have you been diagnosed with a heart disorder?
Client: Yes, Angina Pectoralis.

114

Doctor: ¿El dolor en el pecho le está aumentando?

Cliente: Sí, es cada vez más fuerte.

Doctor: Is your chest pain increasing?

Client: Yes, it's getting worse all the time.

115

Doctor: ¿Ha tomado las medicinas que el doctor le indicó?

Cliente: Sí, pero se me acabaron.

Doctor: Have you been taking the medications your doctor prescribed.

Client: Yes, but I ran out.

116

Doctor: ¿Tiene más de 48 horas con el dolor?

Cliente: No, sólo tengo como 2 horas con el dolor.

Doctor: Have you been in pain more than 48 hours.

Client: No, I' ve only been in pain for 2 hours.

117

Doctor: Usted va a estar bien.

Cliente: Tengo miedo.

Doctor: You will be fine.

Client: I'm scared.

118

Doctor: Respire profundo y cuente hasta 10.

Cliente: 1, 2, 3, 4, 5, 6, 7, 8, 9, 10.

Doctor: Take a deep breath, count to 10.

Client: 1, 2, 3, 4, 5, 6, 7, 8, 9, 10.

119

Doctor: Contrólese por favor.
Cliente: Me siento confundida(o).
Doctor: Please control yourself.
Client: I feel confused.

120

Doctor: Cálmese.
Cliente: No puedo.
Doctor: Relax.
Client: I Can't.

121

Doctor: ¿Se siente cansada(o)?
Cliente: Sí, me siento muy cansada(o).
Doctor: Do you feel tired?
Client: Yes, I feel very tired.

122

Doctor: ¿Se siente débil?
Cliente: Sí, como si me fuera a desmayar.
Doctor: Do you feel weak?
Client: Yes, like I'm about to faint.

123

Doctor: ¿Siente náusea?
Cliente: Sí, y me siento mareada(o).
Doctor: Do you feel nauseous?
Client: Yes, and I feel dizzy.

124

Doctor: ¿Tiene frío?

Cliente: Sí, tengo escalofríos.

Doctor: Are you cold?

Client: Yes, I have chills.

125

Doctor: ¿Está pálida(o)?

Cliente: No sé, pero me siento decaída(o).

Doctor: Are you pale?

Client: I don't know, but I feel weak.

126

Doctor: ¿Se siente confundida(o)?

Cliente: No entiendo.

Doctor: Are you confused?

Client: I don't understand.

127

Doctor: ¿Tiene calor?

Cliente: Sí, me siento muy acalorada(o).

Doctor: Do you feel hot?

Client: Yes, I feel very warm.

128

Doctor: Tome un poco de agua.

Cliente: No quiero, siento ganas de vomitar.

Doctor: Drink some water.

Client: I don't want to, I feel like vomiting.

129

Doctor: ¿Tiene los dedos adormecidos?

Cliente: Sí, y las piernas también.

Doctor: Are your fingers numb?

Client: Yes, and my legs too.

130

Doctor: ¿Siente los labios adormecidos?

Cliente: Sí.

Doctor: Do your lips feel numb?

Client: Yes.

131

Doctor: ¿Tiene dificultad para respirar?

Cliente: No.

Doctor: Are you having any difficulty breathing?

Client: No.

132

Doctor: ¿Tiene dolor en el pecho?

Cliente: No, tengo dolor en la espalda.

Doctor: Do you have chest pain?

Client: No, I have back pain.

133

Doctor: ¿Tiene escalofríos?

Cliente: Sí, tengo mucho frío.

Doctor: Do you have chills?

Client: Yes, I'm very cold.

134

Doctor: No se talle el ojo.
Cliente: Tengo comezón.
Doctor: Don't rub your eyes.
Client: I have an itch.

135

Doctor: Trate de vomitar.
Cliente: No puedo.
Doctor: Try to vomit.
Client: I can't.

136

Doctor: Trate de no vomitar.
Cliente: Siento muchas ganas.
Doctor: Try not to vomit.
Client: I feel like it.

137

Doctor: ¿Le duele el cuello?
Cliente: No, me duele la cabeza.
Doctor: Does your neck hurt?
Client: No, my head hurts.

138

Doctor: ¿Le duele la espalda?
Cliente: Un poco.
Doctor: Does your back hurt.
Client: Just a bit.

139

Doctor: ¿Se tomó algo?

Cliente: Sí, jabón líquido.

Doctor: Did you drink something?

Client: Yes, liquid soap.

140

Doctor: ¿Trató de suicidarse?

Cliente: Sí, se tomó todas las medicinas.

Doctor: Did he (she) try to commit suicide?

Client: Yes, he (she) took all the medications.

Chest and Respiratory
Problemas respiratorios

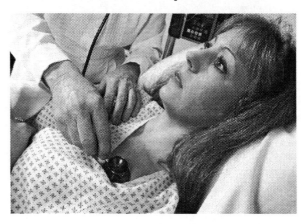

141

Doctor: Buenas tardes, ¿cómo se ha sentido últimamente?

Cliente: No muy bien doctor.

Doctor: Good afternoon. How have you been feeling lately?

Client: Not very well Doctor.

142

Doctor: ¿Tiene dificultad al respirar?

Cliente: Sólo cuando corro mucho.

Doctor: Do you have difficulty breathing?

Client: Only when I run a lot.

143

Doctor: ¿Le duele cuando tose?

Cliente: Mucho.

Doctor: Does it hurt when you cough?

Client: Very much.

144

Doctor: ¿Produce flemas verdes?

Cliente: No, más bien grises.

Doctor: Do you produce green phlegm?

Client: No, more like grey.

145

Doctor: ¿Produce flema gris?

Cliente: Sí, cuando toso.

Doctor: Do you produce grey phlegm?

Client: Yes, when I cough.

146

Doctor: ¿Tiene tos?

Cliente: Sí, constantemente estoy tosiendo.

Doctor: Do you have a cough?

Client: Yes, I am constantly coughing.

147

Doctor: ¿Tiene los senos de la nariz congestionados?

Cliente: No, más bien me escurre mucho la nariz.

Doctor: Is your sinus congested?

Client: No, it's more like I have a runny nose.

148

Doctor: ¿Tiene la nariz tapada?

Cliente: Sí, no puedo respirar.

Doctor: Is your nose all stuffed up?

Client: Yes, I can't breathe.

149

Doctor: ¿Le duele la garganta?
Cliente: No, pero estoy estornudando mucho.
Doctor: Does your throat hurt?
Client: No, but I'm sneezing a lot.

150

Doctor: ¿Está ronca(o)?
Cliente: No, así es mi voz.
Doctor: Are you hoarse?
Client: No, it's my normal voice.

151

Doctor: Usted tiene una infección bacterial.
Cliente: ¿Debo tomar antibiótico?
Doctor: You have a bacterial infection.
Client: Should I take an antibiotic?

152

Doctor: ¿Le escurre la nariz?
Cliente: No, la tengo tapada.
Doctor: Is your nose runny?
Client: No, it's all stuffed up.

153

Doctor: ¿Tiene dolor muscular?
Cliente: Sí, me duele todo el cuerpo.
Doctor: Do you have muscular pain?
Client: Yes, all my body hurts.

154

Doctor: Tome muchos líquidos.
Cliente: Sí doctor.
Doctor: Drink a lot of liquids.
Client: Yes Doctor.

155

Doctor: Usted debe descansar.
Cliente: No puedo, tengo mucho trabajo.
Doctor: You must rest.
Client: But I have a lot of work to do.

156

Doctor: Tome una aspirina.
Cliente: Me irrita el estómago.
Doctor: Take an aspirin.
Client: It upsets my stomach.

157

Doctor: Evite ejercicios fuertes.
Cliente: ¿Puedo salir a correr?
Doctor: Avoid strenuous exercises.
Client: Can I go jogging?

158

Doctor: Lávese las manos varias veces al día.
Cliente: Lo hago antes de cada comida.
Doctor: Wash your hands several times a day.
Client: I do it before every meal.

159

Doctor: Tome un vaso con agua o jugo cada hora.
Cliente: Sí, lo estoy haciendo.
Doctor: Drink a glass of water or juice every hour.
Client: I'm doing that.

160

Doctor: ¿Tiene una tos seca?
Cliente: No, más bien una tos con flema.
Doctor: Do you have a dry cough?
Client: No, more like a cough with phlegm.

161

Doctor: ¿Tiene flema cuando tose?
Cliente: Sí, tengo mucha flema cuando toso.
Doctor: Do you have phlegm when you cough?
Client: Yes, I have lots of phlegm when I cough.

162

Doctor: Usted tiene laringitis.
Cliente: ¿Qué medicina debo tomar?
Doctor: You have laryngitis.
Client: What medication should I take?

163

Doctor: ¿Tiene escalofríos?
Cliente: Por las noches solamente.
Doctor: Do you have chills?
Client: Only at night.

164

Doctor: ¿Le duele el pecho cuando respira profundo?
Cliente: Sí, me duele mucho.
Doctor: Does your chest hurt if you take a deep breath?
Client: Yes, it hurts a lot.

165

Doctor: ¿Se siente muy cansada(o)?
Cliente: Por las tardes.
Doctor: Do you feel tired?
Client: In the afternoon.

166

Doctor: Siga las instrucciones del frasco.
Cliente: No entiendo las instrucciones.
Doctor: Follow the instructions on the bottle.
Client: I don't understand the instructions.

167

Doctor: ¿Tiene inflamadas las anginas?
Cliente: Creo que sí, me duelen mucho.
Doctor: Are your tonsils swollen?
Client: I think so, they hurt a lot.

168

Doctor: Haga gárgaras con agua y sal.
Cliente: ¿Caliente o fría?
Doctor: Gargle with water and salt.
Client: Warm or cold?

Abdominal Problems / Problemas abdominales

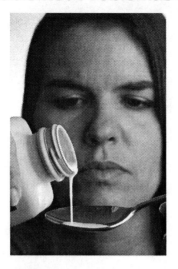

169

Doctor: Buenos días. ¿A qué se debe su visita?

Cliente: Me siento mal.

Doctor: Good morning. What brings you in today?

Client: I'm not feeling well.

170

Doctor: ¿Está estreñida?

Cliente: Sí, me siento muy mal.

Doctor: Are you constipated?

Client: Yes, I feel bad.

171

Doctor: ¿Le duele el abdomen?

Cliente: Sí, del lado derecho.

Doctor: Does your abdomen hurt?

Client: Yes, on the right side.

172

Doctor: ¿Le arde al orinar?
Cliente: Sí, demasiado.
Doctor: Does it burn when you urinate?
Client: Yes, a lot.

173

Doctor: ¿Tiene dificultad al orinar?
Cliente: Sí, orino muy lentamente.
Doctor: Do you have difficulty urinating?
Client: Yes, I urinate too slowly.

174

Doctor: ¿Siente algún tipo de incomodidad en el abdomen?
Cliente: Un poco.
Doctor: Do you feel any sort of abdominal discomfort?
Client: Yes, a little.

175

Doctor: Tome un laxante.
Cliente: ¿Qué tipo me recomienda?
Doctor: Take a laxative
Client: What brand do you recommend?

176

Doctor: ¿Alguien más de su familia tiene los mismos síntomas?
Cliente: Mi hermano(a) y yo solamente.
Doctor: Does anyone in your family have the same symptoms?
Client: Only my brother (sister) and I.

177

Doctor: ¿Alguien más tiene los mismos síntomas?

Cliente: Mi esposo(a) y mi hijo(a).

Doctor: Does anyone else have the same symptoms?

Client: My husband (wife) and my son (daughter).

178

Doctor: Debe dejar de beber alcohol.

Cliente: Pero solamente tomo una copa al día.

Doctor: You must eliminate alcohol.

Client: But I only have one drink a day.

179

Doctor: No tome alcohol.

Cliente: Nunca tomo, no me gusta.

Doctor: Don't drink alcohol.

Client: I never drink it, I don't like it.

Muscles and Bones / Huesos y músculos

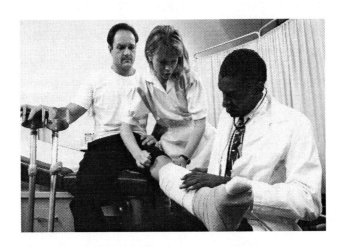

180

Doctor: Buenas tardes, ¿en qué le puedo ayudar?

Cliente: Me siento mal doctor(a).

Doctor: Good afternoon, How can I help you?

Client: I don't feel well, Doctor.

181

Doctor: ¿Le duelen las coyunturas de las manos?

Cliente: Sí, no las puedo mover.

Doctor: Do the jointsin your hands hurt?

Client: Yes, I can't move them.

182

Doctor: ¿Tiene hinchadas las coyunturas?

Cliente: Muy hinchadas doctor(a).

Doctor: Are your joints swollen ?

Client: Very much Doctor.

183

Doctor: ¿Tiene rojo alrededor de las coyunturas?

Cliente: No me he fijado.

Doctor: Do you have redness around your joints?

Client: I haven't noticed.

184

Doctor: ¿Le duele la muñeca?

Cliente: Sí, me dí un golpe.

Doctor: Does your wrist hurt?

Client: Yes, I did hurt myself.

185

Doctor: ¿Siente dificultad al mover las manos?

Cliente: Solamente cuando escribo.

Doctor: Do you have difficulty moving your hands?

Client: Only when I write.

186

Doctor: ¿Siente dificultad al mover las piernas?

Cliente: Por las mañanas solamente.

Doctor: Do you have any difficulty moving your legs?

Client: Only in the mornings.

187

Doctor: ¿Tiene dolores repentinos en el tobillo?

Cliente: Sí, cuando camino largas distancias.

Doctor: Do you have sudden pains in the ankle?

Client: Yes, when I walk a long distance.

188

Doctor: ¿Tiene dolor punzante en el codo?

Cliente: No, más bien en la muñeca.

Doctor: Do you have a sharp pain in your elbow?

Client: No, it's on my wrist.

189

Doctor: ¿Se torció la muñeca?

Cliente: Sí, jugando tenis.

Doctor: Did you twist your wrist?

Client: Yes. While playing tennis.

190

Doctor: Póngase hielo.

Cliente: ¿Por cuánto tiempo?

Doctor: Put some ice on it.

Client: For how long?

191

Doctor: No use zapatos con tacón.

Cliente: Comúnmente uso de tacón bajo.

Doctor: You shoulden't wear high heels.

Client: I usually wear low heels.

192

Doctor: Le recomiendo hacer ejercicios de estiramiento.

Cliente: Tengo muy poco tiempo para hacer ejercicio.

Doctor: I recommend you do stretching exercises.

Client: I have very little time to do exercise.

193

Doctor: Reduzca la actividad.

Cliente: Imposible, tengo que hacer todo mi trabajo.

Doctor: You should cut down on your activities.

Client: It's impossible, I have to get all my work done.

194

Doctor: ¿Tiene calambres?

Cliente: Todas las mañanas.

Doctor: Do you have cramps?

Client: Every morning.

195

Doctor: Tome alimentos altos en potasio.

Cliente: ¿Cuáles son esos?

Doctor: Eat foods high in potassium.

Client: Which ones are those?

196

Doctor: Usted debe de comer más plátanos, papas y tomar jugo de naranja.

Cliente: No me gustan las papas.

Doctor: You should eat more bananas, potatoes and drink orange juice.

Client: I don't like potatoes.

197

Doctor: Dése un masaje en el área afectada.

Cliente: Le pediré a mi esposo(a) que me ayude.

Doctor: Massage the affected area.

Client: I'll ask my husband (wife) to help.

198

Doctor: Usted tiene osteoporosis.

Cliente: ¿Qué medicamentos debo tomar?

Doctor: You have osteoporosis.

Client: What medications should I take?

199

Doctor: Usted debe de tomar más calcio.

Cliente: No me gusta la leche.

Doctor: You must take plenty of calcium.

Client: I don't like milk.

200

Doctor: Tome alimentos lácteos, bajos en grasas.

Cliente: Yo siempre compro leche descremada.

Doctor: Eat dairy products low in fats.

Client: I always buy non fat milk.

201

Doctor: ¿Le duele el talón?

Cliente: Cuando camino solamente.

Doctor: Does your heel hurt?

Client: Only when I walk.

202

Doctor: Tiene que bajar de peso.

Cliente: Sí, pero me cuesta mucho trabajo.

Doctor: You have to lose weight.

Client: Yes, but I have a hard time doing it.

203

Doctor: Use un arco ortopédico dentro del zapato.

Cliente: ¿Dónde lo puedo comprar?

Doctor: Use an orthopedic arch support inside the shoe.

Client: Where can I buy one?

204

Doctor: No corra cuando tenga dolor.

Cliente: Haré ejercicios de estiramiento por alguna temporada.

Doctor: Don't jog if it hurts.

Client: I'll do some stretching exercises for a while.

205

Doctor: Usted tiene una fractura.

Cliente: ¿Me pondrá un yeso?

Doctor: You have a fracture.

Client: Are you going to put on a cast?

206

Doctor: Usted tiene una torcedura.

Cliente: ¿Debo ponerme hielo?

Doctor: You have a sprain.

Client: Should I apply ice?

207

Doctor: Use muletas.

Cliente: ¿Dónde las puedo adquirir?

Doctor: Use crutches.

Client: Where can I find them?

Eyes and Ears / Ojos y oídos

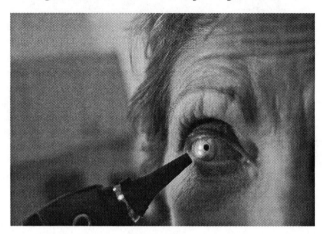

208

Oftalmólogo:	Buenos días. ¿Ha tenido alguna molestia?
Cliente:	Sí, mucha.
Ophthalmologist:	Good morning. Have you had any discomfort?
Client:	Yes, a lot.

209

Oftalmólogo:	¿Tiene comezón en los ojos?
Cliente:	Sí.
Ophthalmologist:	Do your eyes itch?
Client:	Yes.

210

Oftalmólogo:	¿Le salen lagañas?
Cliente:	Constantemente.
Ophthalmologist:	Do you have a discharge from your eyes?
Client:	Constantly.

211

Oftalmólogo:	Usted tiene conjuntivitis.
Cliente:	Me duelen los ojos doctora(or).
Ophthalmologist:	You have conjunctivitis.
Client:	My eyes hurt, doctor.

212

Oftalmólogo:	Le vamos a hacer una prueba de glaucoma.
Cliente:	¿Toma mucho tiempo ?
Ophthalmologist:	We are going to do a glaucoma test.
Client:	Will it take long?

213

Oftalmólogo:	Usted tiene glaucoma.
Cliente:	¿Qué tan grave es?
Ophthalmologist:	You have glaucoma.
Client:	Is it very serious?

214

Oftalmólogo:	¿Tiene la vista borrosa?
Cliente:	Un poco, pero con los lentes se mejora.
Ophthalmologist:	Is your sight blurred?
Client:	A bit, but it improves with my glasses on.

215

Oftalmólogo:	¿Se lastimó el ojo?
Cliente:	Sí, jugando con la pelota.
Ophthalmologist:	Did you hurt your eye?
Client:	Yes, while playing ball.

216

Oftalmólogo:	¿Le duele el oído?
Cliente:	Sí, mucho.
Ophthalmologist:	Does your ear hurt?
Client:	Yes, very much.

217

Oftalmólogo:	¿Le sale secreción del oído?
Cliente:	Sí, desde hace una semana.
Ophthalmologist:	Do you have any fluid coming out of your ear?
Client:	Yes, for a week now.

218

Oftalmólogo:	¿Siente el oído tapado?
Cliente:	Sí, pero siempre lo he sentido así.
Ophthalmologist:	Does your ear feel blocked?
Client:	Yes, It has always felt that way.

219

Oftalmólogo:	¿Siente que trae algo dentro del oído?
Cliente:	Sí, algo me molesta.
Ophthalmologist:	Do you feel as if you had something in your ear?
Client:	Yes, something is bothering me.

220

Oftalmólogo:	¿Escucha bien?
Cliente:	No, me siento como sordo(a).
Ophthalmologist:	Can you hear well?
Client:	No, I feel like I'm deaf.

221

Oftalmólogo:	¿Escucha un zumbido?
Cliente:	Constantemente doctora(or).
Ophthalmologist:	Do you hear a buzz?
Client:	Constantly Doctor.

222

Oftalmólogo:	Usted tiene una infección en el oído.
Cliente:	¿En cuánto tiempo se me quitará?
Ophthalmologist:	You have an infection in your ear.
Client:	How long will it last?

Headaches and Tension / Jaqueca y tensión

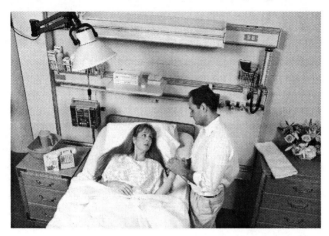

223

Doctor: Pase usted, ¿cómo ha estado?
Cliente: No muy bien doctor (a).
Doctor: Come in. How have you been?
Client: Not very well, Doctor.

224

Doctor: ¿Está usted bajo alguna tensión?
Cliente: Sí, mucha.
Doctor: Are you under any pressure?
Client: Yes, a lot.

225

Doctor: ¿Le duele la cabeza?
Cliente: Sí, desde ayer.
Doctor: Do you have a headache?
Client: Yes, since yesterday.

226

Doctor: ¿Había tenido un dolor de cabeza así?

Cliente: Nunca doctora(or).

Doctor: Have you ever had a headache like this one?

Client: Never, doctor.

227

Doctor: ¿Siente punzadas en la cabeza?

Cliente: Sí, en la frente.

Doctor: Do you have sharp headache pains?

Client: Yes, in my forehead.

228

Doctor: ¿Siente el cuello entumido?

Cliente: Sí, no puedo voltear la cabeza.

Doctor: Does your neck feel numb?

Client: Yes, I can't move my neck.

229

Doctor: ¿Ha perdido la coordinación?

Cliente: Sí.

Doctor: Have you lost your coordination?

Client: Yes.

230

Doctor: ¿Se dió un golpe en la cabeza?

Cliente: Sí, pero nunca pensé que fuera de gravedad.

Doctor: Did you hit your head?

Client: Yes, but I never thought it was serious.

231

Doctor: ¿Le duele la cabeza por las mañanas?

Cliente: Sí, cuando me levanto.

Doctor: Does your head hurt in the mornings.

Client: Yes, when I get up.

232

Doctor: ¿Le duele la quijada?

Cliente: No, solamente el cuello.

Doctor: Does your jaw hurt?

Client: No, only my neck hurts.

233

Doctor: ¿Le duelen el cuello y los hombros?

Cliente: No, solamente la quijada.

Doctor: Do your neck and shoulders hurt?

Client: No, only my jaw.

234

Doctor: ¿Ha estado expuesto a vapores químicos, como pintura?

Cliente: Solamente insecticidas doctora (or).

Doctor: Have you been exposed to chemical fumes, like paint?

Client: Only insecticides, doctor.

235

Doctor: ¿Le duele la cabeza desde que empezó a tomar la medicina?

Cliente: No, me siento mejor.

Doctor: Does your head hurt since you began taking this medicine?

Client: No, I feel better.

236

Doctor: ¿Ha tomado medicamentos para el dolor de cabeza?

Cliente: Aspirinas y otros analgésicos.

Doctor: Have you been taking any medications for the headache?

Client: Aspirin and other pain killers.

237

Doctor: ¿Sufre de migraña?

Cliente: No, no he tenido un dolor de cabeza en mucho tiempo.

Doctor: Do you suffer from migraine?

Client: No, I haven't had a headache in a long time.

238

Doctor: Recuéstese y apague la luz.

Cliente: ¿Por cuánto tiempo?

Doctor: Lie back and turn off the lights.

Client: For how long?

239

Doctor: Relájese.

Cliente: Me cuesta trabajo.

Doctor: Relax.

Client: It's hard for me.

240

Doctor: Haga ejercicios de relajación.

Cliente: Los hago todas la mañanas.

Doctor: Do relaxation exercises.

Client: I do them every morning.

241

Doctor: Reduzca la tensión emocional.
Cliente: Pero mi situación es muy difícil.
Doctor: Reduce emotional tension.
Client: But with my situation it's so difficult.

242

Doctor: Reduzca la tensión física.
Cliente: ¿Cómo puedo lograrlo?
Doctor: Reduce physical tension.
Client: How can I do that?

243

Doctor: Corrija su postura.
Cliente: Trataré.
Doctor: Improve your posture.
Client: I'll try.

244

Doctor: Respire profundo.
Cliente: ¿Esto me ayudará a relajarme?
Doctor: Take a deep breath.
Client: Will this help me relax?

245

Doctor: Dése un masaje en el cuello y la espalda.
Cliente: Iré con un masajista profesional.
Doctor: Get a neck and back massage.
Client: I'll go to a professional masseuse.

Doctor: Tome un baño de tina.

Cliente: Bien.

Doctor: Take a bath.

Client: Fine.

Skin / Piel

247

Médico: Pásele. ¿Cómo se siente hoy?

Cliente: Bien doctora (or), pero...

Doctor: Come in, How are you feeling today?

Client: Fine Doctor, but...

248

Médico: Usted tiene un problema de acné.

Cliente: ¿Cómo lo puedo eliminar?

Doctor: You have an acne problem.

Client: How can I get rid of it?

249

Médico: ¿Está usted tomando anticonceptivos?

Cliente: Sí.

Doctor: Are you taking any contraceptives?

Client: Yes.

250

Médico: Lávese la cara con jabón de avena.

Cliente: ¿Dónde lo puedo encontrar?

Doctor: Wash your face with oatmeal soap.

Client: Where can I find it?

251

Médico: Lávese la cara con peróxido de benzol.

Cliente: ¿No me harán daño los químicos?

Doctor: Wash your face with benzol peroxide.

Client: Could the chemicals hurt me?

252

Médico: ¿Le picó un insecto?

Cliente: Creo que sí.

Doctor: Did you get an insect bite?

Client: I believe so.

253

Médico: Tiene un grano.

Cliente: Me duele un poco.

Doctor: You have a pimple.

Client: It hurts a little.

254

Médico: Puede ser una infección.

Cliente: ¿Usted cree?

Doctor: It could be an infection.

Client: Do you believe so?

255

Médico: Es una erupción cutánea.
Cliente: La tengo desde el martes.
Doctor: It's a skin eruption.
Client: I have had it since Tuesday.

256

Médico: ¿Ha cambiado de forma el lunar?
Cliente: No que me haya dado cuenta.
Doctor: Has the shape of the mole changed?
Client: Not that I have noticed.

257

Médico: ¿Ha cambiado de tamaño el lunar?
Cliente: Sí, últimamente.
Doctor: Has the size of the mole changed?
Client: Yes, recently.

258

Médico: ¿Le duele el lunar?
Cliente: Solamente si lo toco.
Doctor: Does the mole hurt?
Client: Only if I touch it.

259

Médico: ¿Está el lunar constantemente irritado?
Cliente: No, no me duele.
Doctor: Is the mole constantly irritated?
Client: No, it doesn't hurt.

260

Médico: ¿Tiene irritación en las piernas?

Cliente: Sí, apareció recientemente.

Doctor: Do you have a rash on your legs?

Client: Yes, I got it recently.

261

Médico: Usted tiene impétigo.

Cliente: ¿Qué es eso?

Doctor: You have impetigo.

Client: What is that?

262

Médico: ¿Tiene comezón en la cabeza?

Cliente: No, pero estoy perdiendo el pelo.

Doctor: Does your scalp itch?

Client: No but I'm losing hair.

263

Médico: ¿Tiene la piel reseca?

Cliente: Sí, ¿me recomienda una crema humectante?

Doctor: Is your skin dry?

Client: Yes, would you recommend a moisturizer?

264

Médico: No se exprima los granos, pueden infectarse.

Cliente: ¿Me puede quedar una cicatriz?

Doctor: Don't squeeze your pimples, they could get infected.

Client: Could it leave a scar?

265

Médico: Este producto lo venden en cualquier farmacia.

Cliente: ¿Cuál es la más cercana?

Doctor: This product is sold in any pharmacy.

Client: Where is the nearest one?

266

Médico: Aplíqueselo diario después de lavarse.

Cliente: ¿Qué cantidad?

Doctor: Apply it daily after washing.

Client: For how long?

267

Médico: Va a tomar varias semanas para hacer efecto.

Cliente: ¿Cuántas?

Doctor: It's going to take several weeks to take effect.

Client: How many?

268

Médico: ¿Tiene una ampolla?

Cliente: Sí, un poco grande.

Doctor: Do you have a blister?

Client: Yes, and it's a big one.

269

Médico: Evite los zapatos apretados.

Cliente: Son los únicos que tengo.

Doctor: Avoid tight shoes.

Client: These are the only ones I have.

270

Médico: Lave el área con agua y jabón.

Cliente: ¿Qué tan frecuentemente?

Doctor: Wash the area with water and soap.

Client: How often?

271

Médico: Póngase una crema antibiótica.

Cliente: ¿Me dará una receta?

Doctor: Apply an antibiotic cream.

Client: Will you give me a prescription?

272

Médico: No se ponga alcohol.

Cliente: ¿Qué debo usar?

Doctor: Don't apply alcohol.

Client: What should I use instead?

273

Médico: Cambie la venda una vez al día.

Cliente: Necesito ayuda para hacerlo.

Doctor: Change the bandage once a day.

Client: I need help to do it.

274

Médico: Quítese la venda antes de acostarse.

Cliente: De acuerdo.

Doctor: Remove the bandage before going to bed.

Client: All right.

275

Médico: Aplique calor sobre el área afectada.
Cliente: ¿Con toallas calientes?
Doctor: Apply heat over the affected area.
Client: With warm towels?

276

Médico: ¿Le duele mucho?
Cliente: No, pero es incómodo.
Doctor: Does it hurt a lot?
Client: No but it's uncomfortable.

277

Médico: ¿El dolor limita sus actividades?
Cliente: Sí, no puedo caminar.
Doctor: Does the pain limit your activities?
Client: Yes, I can't walk.

278

Médico: Usted tiene caspa.
Cliente: Sí, el shampoo no me sirve.
Doctor: You have dandruff.
Client: Yes, the shampoo doesn't help.

279

Médico: Use shampoo anticaspa.
Cliente: ¿De qué marca?
Doctor: Use dandruff shampoo.
Client: What brand?

280

Médico: Evite los baños calientes.
Cliente: Así lo haré.
Doctor: Avoid hot baths.
Client: I'll do that.

281

Médico: Use crema de cortisona.
Cliente: ¿Qué tan seguido debo usarla?
Doctor: Use cortisone cream.
Client: How often should I use it?

282

Médico: Evite la ropa de lana.
Cliente: ¿Es mejor la de algodón?
Doctor: Avoid wool clothing.
Client: Is cotton better?

283

Médico: Use ropa de algodón.
Cliente: ¿Debe de ser 100% de algodón?
Doctor: Use cotton clothing.
Client: Must it be 100% cotton?

284

Médico: Evite detergentes y desodorantes.
Cliente: Sí, he notado que eso me afecta.
Doctor: Avoid detergents and deodorants.
Client: Yes, I have noticed this affects me.

285

Médico: Evite los perfumes y lociones.

Cliente: ¿Por completo?

Doctor: Avoid perfumes and lotions.

Client: Completely?

286

Médico: Evite exponerse al sol.

Cliente: Usaré sombrero de hoy en adelante.

Doctor: Avoid exposure to the sun.

Client: I will use a hat from now on.

287

Médico: Use crema protectora del sol.

Cliente: ¿Qué marca?

Doctor: Use sun screen.

Client: What brand?

288

Médico: No se bañe todos los días.

Cliente: ¿Cada cuánto debo de bañarme?

Doctor: Don't shower every day.

Client: How often should I shower?

289

Médico: Use muy poco jabón.

Cliente: ¿Algún tipo en especial?

Doctor: Use very little soap.

Client: Any special kind?

290

Médico: Use sandalias.

Cliente: Sí, tengo unas.

Doctor: Wear sandals.

Client: Yes, I have some.

291

Médico: Use calcetines de algodón.

Cliente: Sí, he notado que son mejores.

Doctor: Use cotton socks.

Client: Yes, I noticed that they are better.

292

Médico: Póngase talco para absorber la humedad.

Cliente: De acuerdo.

Doctor: Use powder to absorb moisture.

Client: I will.

293

Médico: Usted tiene urticaria.

Cliente: ¿Se quita?

Doctor: You have hives.

Client: Will they go away?

294

Médico: Es una reacción a algo que comió.

Cliente: ¿Que habrá sido?

Doctor: It's a reaction to something you have eaten.

Client: What could it have been?

295

Médico: Es una reacción a la medicina.

Cliente: ¿A cuál de ellas?

Doctor: It's a reaction to the medicine.

Client: Which one?

296

Médico: Aplique bolsas de hielo.

Cliente: ¿Durante cuánto tiempo?

Doctor: Put on a cold pack.

Client: For how long?

297

Médico: Remoje el área con agua caliente.

Cliente: ¿Por cuánto tiempo?

Doctor: Soak the area with hot water.

Client: For how long?

298

Médico: Lave sábanas y toallas con agua caliente.

Cliente: Siempre lo hago.

Doctor: Wash blankets and towels with hot water.

Client: I always do it.

299

Médico: ¿Comió algo a lo que pudiera ser alérgico?

Cliente: Sí, camarones.

Doctor: Did you eat something that you're allergic to?

Client: Yes, shrimp.

300

Médico: ¿Está usted tomando alguna medicina?
Cliente: Solamente jarabe para la tos.
Doctor: Are you taking any medications?
Client: Only cough syrup.

301

Médico: ¿Ha estado usted bajo tensión?
Cliente: No más de lo común.
Doctor: Have you been under any tension?
Client: Not more than usual.

302

Médico: ¿Le duelen las coyunturas?
Cliente: No, me siento muy bien de eso.
Doctor: Do your joints hurt?
Client: No, I'm fine there.

303

Médico: ¿Tiene comezón?
Cliente: Sí, desde que empecé a tomar la medicina.
Doctor: Do you itch?
Client: Yes, since I started taking the medication.

304

Médico: ¿La urticaria se está expandiendo?
Cliente: Creo que un poco.
Doctor: Is the rash getting worse?
Client: A little bit, I think so.

305

Médico: Use detergentes hipoalergénicos.

Cliente: ¿Cómo cuáles?

Doctor: Use hypoallergenic detergents.

Client: Like which ones?

306

Médico: Use talco para bebés.

Cliente: Así lo haré.

Doctor: Use baby powder.

Client: O.K.

307

Médico: ¿Pasa mucho tiempo expuesto al sol?

Cliente: Sí, por el trabajo.

Doctor: Do you spend a lot of time exposed to the sun?

Client: Yes, due to my job.

308

Médico: ¿El lunar le sangra?

Cliente: Ya no tanto.

Doctor: Does the mole bleed?

Client: Not as much.

309

Médico: ¿El lunar le está creciendo poco a poco?

Cliente: No, ha estado así desde que recuerdo.

Doctor: Is the mole growing a bit at a time?

Client: No, it has been like this since I remember.

310

Médico: Déjeme ver el lunar.

Cliente: ¿Cuál?

Doctor: Let me see the mole.

Client: Which one?

311

Médico: Use crema con factor de protección solar mayor de 15.

Cliente: ¿Cualquier marca es buena?

Doctor: Use sun screen with SPF higher than 15.

Client: Will any brand do?

312

Médico: Tome baños de agua fría.

Cliente: ¿Qué tan seguido?

Doctor: Take a cold shower.

Client: How often?

Back and Neck / Espalda y cuello

313

Doctor: Adelante, ¿Cómo ha estado?

Cliente: Todavía me siento mal.

Doctor: Come in. How are you?

Client: I still feel bad.

314

Doctor: ¿Por cuánto tiempo le ha dolido la espalda?

Cliente: Ya tiene mucho tiempo.

Doctor: How long have you had this back pain?

Client: For a long time.

315

Doctor: ¿Cuánto tiempo tiene con este dolor?

Cliente: Ayer me empezó.

Doctor: How long have you had this pain?

Client: Since yesterday.

316

Doctor: ¿Se lastimó de alguna manera?

Cliente: Sí, me caí.

Doctor: Did you hurt yourself in any way?

Client: Yes, I fell down.

317

Doctor: ¿Le duele la pierna?

Cliente: A veces.

Doctor: Does your leg hurt?

Client: Sometimes.

318

Doctor: ¿Sufre de artritis?

Cliente: No me la han diagnosticado.

Doctor: Do you suffer from arthritis?

Client: I have not been diagnosed with it.

319

Doctor: No levante objetos pesados.

Cliente: De acuerdo.

Doctor: Don't lift heavy objects.

Client: Fine.

320

Doctor: Haga ejercicios de estiramiento.

Cliente: ¿Qué tan seguido?

Doctor: Do stretching exercises.

Client: How often?

321

Doctor: ¿Le duele el cuello?

Cliente: Sólo cuando volteo.

Doctor: Does your neck hurt?

Client: Only when I turn.

322

Doctor: Asuma una postura correcta.

Cliente: ¿A qué se refiere?

Doctor: Stand up straight.

Client: What do you mean?

323

Doctor: Haga ejercicios de relajación.

Cliente: ¿Cómo se hacen?

Doctor: Do relaxation exercises.

Client: How do you do them?

324

Doctor: No haga ejercicios que le causen dolor.

Cliente: Así lo haré.

Doctor: Don't do exercises that cause you pain.

Client: I'll do that.

Men's issues / Temas masculinos

325

Doctor: Si toma, no maneje.

Cliente: No lo hago.

Doctor: If you drink, don't drive.

Client: I never do.

326

Doctor: Póngase el cinturón de seguridad.

Cliente: Siempre lo hago.

Doctor: Wear your seat belt.

Client: I always do.

327

Doctor: ¿Tiene problemas de erección?

Cliente: Hasta el momento no.

Doctor: Do you have erection problems?

Client: Not up til now.

328

Doctor: Fortalezca su abdomen con ejercicios.

Cliente: Me inscribiré en un gimnasio.

Doctor: Strengthen your abdomen with exercises.

Client: I will join a gym.

329

Doctor: Usted tiene una infección en la próstata.

Cliente: ¿Cómo la pude haber contraído?

Doctor: You have a prostate infection.

Client: How could I have gotten it?

330

Doctor: ¿Le arde al orinar?

Cliente: No, pero tardo mucho.

Doctor: Does it burn when you urinate?

Client: No, but it takes too long.

331

Doctor: ¿Le arde al eyacular?

Cliente: No he sentido ese problema.

Doctor: Does it burn when you ejaculate?

Client: I have not noticed that problem.

332

Doctor: ¿Tiene dificultad para orinar?

Cliente: Sí, siento la urgencia pero no puedo.

Doctor: Do you have difficulty urinating?

Client: Yes, I feel the urge but I can't go.

333

Doctor: ¿Siente que no puede orinar?

Cliente: No, ese problema no lo tengo.

Doctor: Do you feel you can't urinate?

Client: No, I don't have that problem.

334

Doctor: ¿Sufre de incontinencia?

Cliente: Sí, desde que salí de la cirugía.

Doctor: Do you suffer from incontinence?

Client: Yes, since I came out of surgery.

335

Doctor: ¿Está tomando diuréticos?

Cliente: Sí, para adelgazar.

Doctor: Are you taking diuretics?

Client: Yes, to lose weight.

336

Doctor: ¿Está usted tomando antiestamínicos?

Cliente: Desde que me comenzó la gripa.

Doctor: Are you taking antihistamines?

Client: Since I got this cold.

337

Doctor: ¿Está tomando antidepresivos?

Cliente: Sí, el siquiatra me los recetó.

Doctor: Are you taking antidepressants?

Client: Yes, the psychiatrist prescribed them.

338

Doctor: Esto puede agravar el problema urinario.

Cliente: ¿Debo de suspender algún medicamento?

Doctor: This could worsen the urinary problem.

Client: Should I stop taking any medications?

339

Doctor: ¿Le han diagnosticado cáncer en la próstata?

Cliente: Nunca me han hecho una prueba.

Doctor: Have you been diagnosed with prostrate cancer?

Client: I never had the test done.

340

Doctor: Le vamos a hacer un examen de la próstata.

Cliente: ¿Hoy mismo?

Doctor: We are going to do a prostate test.

Client: Today?

Women's Issues / Temas femeninos

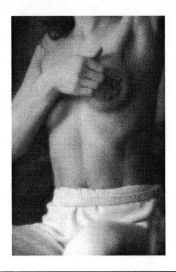

341

Doctor: Buenas tardes. ¿Cómo se ha sentido?

Cliente: No muy bien doctor(a).

Doctor: Good afternoon. How have you been feeling?

Client: Not very well Doctor.

342

Doctor: Usted debe hacerse un mamograma.

Cliente: ¿Debo de hacer una cita?

Doctor: You should have a mammogram.

Client: Should I make an appointment?

343

Doctor: El cáncer de pecho no es común en las mujeres menores de 40 años.

Cliente: ¿Cuándo debo de hacerme un mamograma?

Doctor: Breast cancer is not common in women under 40.

Client: When should I have an exam?

344

Doctor: Autoexamine sus pechos.

Cliente: ¿Cómo debo de hacerlo?

Doctor: Do a self exam of your breast.

Client: How should I do it?

345

Doctor: Si nota algún cambio venga a verme.

Cliente: ¿Tengo que hacer cita?

Doctor: If you notice a change come and see me.

Client: Do I need to make an appointment?

346

Doctor: ¿Ha cambiado el tamaño de sus pechos?

Cliente: Creo que sí.

Doctor: Has the size of your breast changed?

Client: Yes, I think so.

347

Doctor: Ha cambiado la forma de sus pechos.

Cliente: Sí, mucho.

Doctor: Has the shape of your breast changed?

Client: Yes, very much.

348

Doctor: ¿Tiene secreciones del pezón?

Cliente: Sólo durante el amamantamiento.

Doctor: Does your nipple secrete?

Client: Only during breast feeding.

349

Doctor: Examine sus pechos usando la yema de los dedos.

Cliente: ¿Qué debo buscar?

Doctor: Examine your breast with the tips of your fingers.

Client: What should I look for?

350

Doctor: La mayoría de los endurecimientos no son malignos.

Cliente: ¿Comó se puede determinar?

Doctor: Most lumps are not malignant.

Client: How can that be determined?

351

Doctor: El mamograma es una radiografía del pecho.

Cliente: ¿Qué tan confiable es?

Doctor: A mammogram is an x-ray of the breast.

Client: How reliable is it?

352

Doctor: Debe de hacerse un mamograma cada 3 años.

Cliente: Lo haré.

Doctor: You should have a mammogram every 3 years.

Client: I will.

353

Doctor: Hágase cada mes en casa un autoexamen de sus pechos.

Cliente: ¿Me puede dar las instrucciones de cómo hacerlo?

Doctor: Do a self examination of your breast once a month at home.

Client: Can you give me the instructions on how to do it?

354

Doctor: ¿Tiene alguna molestia en la vagina?

Cliente: Sí, tengo un desecho.

Doctor: Do you have any discomfort in your vagina?

Client: Yes I have a discharge.

355

Doctor: ¿Tiene secreciones amarillas?

Cliente: Sí, por eso vine a verlo.

Doctor: Do you have a yellow discharge?

Client: Yes, that is why I came to see you.

356

Doctor: ¿Tiene secreciones blancas?

Cliente: Sí, últimamente.

Doctor: Do you have a white discharge?

Client: Yes, lately.

357

Doctor: ¿Siente dolor al orinar?

Cliente: Sí, me arde mucho.

Doctor: Does it hurt when you urinate?

Client: Yes, it burns a lot.

358

Doctor: ¿La orina tiene un olor fuerte?

Cliente: No lo he notado.

Doctor: Does the urine have a strong odor?

Client: I have not noticed any.

359

Doctor: La prueba del Papanicolau sirve para detectar el cáncer cervical.

Cliente: ¿Cada cuándo debe hacerse?

Doctor: A Pap test is to identify cervical cancer.

Client: How often should it be done?

360

Doctor: Puede tener cierta incomodidad.

Cliente: ¿Me va a doler mucho?

Doctor: It may be uncomfortable.

Client: Will it hurt a lot?

361

Doctor: Le va a doler un poco.

Cliente: ¿Va a durar mucho tiempo?

Doctor: It's going to hurt a little.

Client: Is this going to take long?

362

Doctor: Hágame saber si siente dolor.

Cliente: Sí, me está doliendo mucho.

Doctor: Let me know if you feel pain.

Client: Yes, it is hurting a lot.

363

Doctor: Haga una cita para su examen médico.

Cliente: ¿Para qué fecha?

Doctor: Make an appointment for your medical exam.

Client: For what date?

364

Doctor: Haga su cita dos semanas después de su período.

Cliente: Voy a estar de vacaciones.

Doctor: Make the appointment for two weeks after your period.

Client: I'm going to be out on vacation.

365

Doctor: Haga su cita una semana después de su período.

Cliente: Ese día no puedo.

Doctor: Make your appointment one week after your period.

Client: I can't come that day.

366

Doctor: ¿Es usted diabética(o)?

Cliente: No, que yo sepa.

Doctor: Are you diabetic?

Client: Not that I know of.

367

Doctor: ¿Tiene usted presión alta?

Cliente: Sí, es común en mi familia.

Doctor: Do you have high blood pressure?

Client: Yes, it is common in my family.

368

Doctor: ¿Sufre usted de convulsiones?

Cliente: Sí, me dan con frecuencia.

Doctor: Do you suffer from convulsions?

Client: Yes, I have them frequently.

369

Doctor: ¿Tiene usted alguna enfermedad hereditaria?

Cliente: Ninguna, pero en mi familia hay diabéticos.

Doctor: Do you have any hereditary illness?

Client: No, but some of my family are diabetic.

370

Doctor: Necesita tomar medicamentos especiales durante el embarazo.

Cliente: ¿De qué tipo?

Doctor: You need to take some special medications during pregnancy.

Client: What kind?

371

Doctor: Mantenga una dieta balanceada.

Cliente: ¿Tiene alguna recomendación?

Doctor: Keep a balanced diet.

Client: Do you have any recommendations?

372

Doctor: ¿Cuándo fue su último período?

Cliente: La semana pasada.

Doctor: When was your last period?

Client: Last week.

373

Doctor: Hágase una prueba de embarazo en casa.

Cliente: ¿Es confiable?

Doctor: Do a pregnancy test at home.

Client: Is it reliable?

374

Doctor: Hágase una prueba de enfermedades venéreas.

Cliente: ¿Creé que sea necesario?

Doctor: Have a venereal disease test done.

Client: Do you believe it is necessary?

375

Doctor: ¿Se siente mareada?

Cliente: Sí, últimamente.

Doctor: Do you feel dizzy?

Client: Yes, lately.

376

Doctor: Haga 6 pequeñas comidas al día.

Cliente: ¿Por cuánto tiempo?

Doctor: Have 6 small meals a day.

Client: For how long?

377

Doctor: Incluya proteína en cada comida.

Cliente: Estoy comiendo carne y pescado. ¿Está bién?

Doctor: Include protein in each meal.

Client: I'm eating fish and meat. Is that OK?

378

Doctor: Coma galletas o pan tostado por las mañanas después de levantarse.

Cliente: ¿Esto para qué sirve?

Doctor: Eat crackers and toast before getting up in the mornings.

Client: What is that good for?

379

Doctor: Tome vitamina B6.

Cliente: ¿Me recomienda algún suplemento vitamínico?

Doctor: Take Vitamin B6.

Client: Will you recommend a vitamin supplement?

380

Doctor: Coma más cereal, germen de trigo y nueces.

Cliente: Así lo haré.

Doctor: Eat more cereal, wheat germ and nuts.

Client: I'll do that.

381

Doctor: Mantenga una actitud positiva.

Cliente: Me es difícil.

Doctor: Keep a positive attitude.

Client: It is hard for me.

382

Doctor: Evite bebidas con cafeína.

Cliente: ¿Los refrescos también?

Doctor: Avoid drinks containing caffeine.

Client: Soft drinks also?

383

Doctor: No se ponga zapatos de tacón alto.

Cliente: Está bien.

Doctor: Don't wear high heel shoes.

Client: I'll do so.

384

Doctor: Evite deportes de alto riesgo.

Cliente: ¿Puedo nadar?

Doctor: Avoid high risk sports.

Client: Can I swim?

385

Doctor: Tome alimentos altos en calcio.

Cliente: Tomo mucha leche.

Doctor: Eat foods high in calcium.

Client: I drink a lot of milk.

386

Doctor: Controle su peso.

Cliente: ¿Cuánto debo pesar?

Doctor: Control your weight.

Client: How much should I weigh?

387

Doctor: Tome clases de preparación para el parto.

Cliente: ¿En dónde me inscribo?

Doctor: Take childbirth classes.

Client: Where can I enroll?

388

Doctor: Mantenga un buen sentido del humor.

Cliente: Siempre lo hago.

Doctor: Keep a good sense of humor.

Client: I always do that.

389

Doctor: Usted necesita una cirugía especial.

Cliente: ¿De qué tipo?

Doctor: You need a special surgery.

Client: What kind?

390

Doctor: ¿Sangra entre períodos?

Cliente: Sí, siempre.

Doctor: Do you bleed between periods?

Client: Yes, always.

391

Doctor: ¿Tiene usted un dispositivo intrauterino?

Cliente: No, me lo quitaron.

Doctor: Do you have an IUD?

Client: No, I had it removed.

392

Doctor: El sangrado es normal durante los primeros meses.

Cliente: ¿Cuánto debe durar?

Doctor: Bleeding is normal during the first months.

Client: How long should this last?

393

Doctor: Es normal cuando se está dando pecho.

Cliente: ¿Se quita después?

Doctor: It is normal during breast feeding.

Client: Will it go away later?

394

Doctor: ¿Le duele cuando sangra?

Cliente: Sí, tengo un dolor punzante.

Doctor: Does it hurt when you bleed?

Client: Yes, I have a sharp pain.

395

Doctor: ¿Sangra después de tener relaciones sexuales?

Cliente: No. Solamente durante el período.

Doctor: Do you bleed after intercourse?

Client: No, only during my period.

396

Doctor: ¿Tiene períodos menstruales irregulares?

Cliente: Siempre he sido irregular.

Doctor: Do you have irregular menstrual periods?

Client: I have always been irregular.

397

Doctor: ¿Ha tenido cambios de conducta?

Cliente: No que lo haya notado.

Doctor: Have you had behavioral changes?

Client: Not that I have noticed.

398

Doctor: El período menstrual es diferente en todas las mujeres.

Cliente: ¿En qué consiste?

Doctor: The menstrual periods are different in all women.

Client: In what way?

399

Doctor: ¿Le dan bochornos repentinos?

Cliente: Últimamente sí.

Doctor: Do you get sudden hot flashes?

Client: Yes, lately

400

Doctor: ¿Tiene resequedad en la vagina?

Cliente: Sí, es muy incómodo.

Doctor: Do you have vaginal dryness?

Client: Yes, it is very uncomfortable.

401

Doctor: ¿Sufre de insomnio?

Cliente: No todas las noches.

Doctor: Do you suffer from insomnia?

Client: Not every night.

402

Doctor: ¿Se siente deprimida?

Cliente: Un poco. Pero creo que es por otra razón.

Doctor: Do you feel depressed?

Client: A little, but I think it is for another reason.

403

Doctor: ¿Se siente nerviosa?

Cliente: Constantemente.

Doctor: Do you feel nervous?

Client: Constantly.

404

Doctor: ¿Se siente cansada?

Cliente: Sí, durante todo el día.

Doctor: Do you feel tired?

Client: Yes, all day long.

405

Doctor: Mantenga un registro de sus períodos.

Cliente: ¿Qué es lo que debo de anotar?

Doctor: Keep a record of your periods.

Client: What should I record?

406

Doctor: Usted necesita una terapia hormonal.

Cliente: ¿Por cuánto tiempo la debo tomar?

Doctor: You need hormone therapy.

Client: For how long must I take them?

407

Doctor: ¿Tiene flujo abundante durante la menstruación?

Cliente: Sí, y cólicos muy fuertes.

Doctor: Do you have a heavy flow during menstruation?

Client: Yes, and strong menstrual cramps.

408

Doctor: ¿Su ciclo menstrual dura menos de 21 días?

Cliente: Sí, dura solamente 18 días.

Doctor: Is your menstrual cycle less than 21 days?

Client: Yes, it's every 18 days.

409

Doctor: ¿Sospecha que su dolor lo causa el DIU?

Cliente: Creo que sí.

Doctor: Do you suspect the IUD is causing this pain?

Client: I believe so.

410

Doctor: ¿Ha tenido diarrea, fiebre o reacciones en la piel?

Cliente: Ninguna.

Doctor: Have you had diarrhea, fever or skin reactions?

Client: None.

411

Doctor: ¿Ha tenido dolor menstrual más fuerte que el de costumbre?

Cliente: Éste último período, sí.

Doctor: Have you had stronger menstrual cramps than usual?

Client: This last period, yes.

412

Doctor: ¿Se le pasó su período menstrual?

Cliente: Sí, creo que estoy embarazada.

Doctor: Have you missed your period?

Client: Yes, I believe I'm pregnant.

413

Doctor: ¿Ha perdido peso?

Cliente: No, más bien he aumentado.

Doctor: Have you lost weight?

Client: No, I have gained instead

414

Doctor: ¿Qué clase de anticonceptivos toma?

Cliente: No estoy tomando ninguno.

Doctor: What kind of contraceptives do you take?

Client: I'm not taking any.

415

Doctor: ¿Qué clase de protección utiliza?

Cliente: Uso preservativos.

Doctor: What kind of protection do you use?

Client: I use condoms.

416

Doctor: Aprenda a relajarse.

Cliente: ¿Cuál es la mejor manera?

Doctor: Learn to relax.

Client: What is the best way?

417

Doctor: Usted tiene el síndrome premenstrual.

Cliente: Me lo imaginaba.

Doctor: You have PMS (Pre-menstrual syndrome)

Client: I thought so.

418

Doctor: ¿Aún le duelen los pechos?

Cliente: No, ya me siento mejor.

Doctor: Do your breasts still hurt?

Client: No, I feel better now.

419
___

Doctor: Usted está reteniendo líquidos.

Cliente: Sí, sigo aumentando de peso.

Doctor: You are retaining fluids.

Client: Yes, I keep gaining weight.

Children's Health / Salud y niños

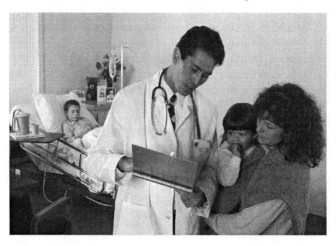

420

Pediatra:	El cordón umbilical se desprende entre la primera y la tercera semana.
Cliente:	¿Le traigo al (a la) niño(a) cuando se le desprenda?
Pediatrician:	The umbilical cord will drop off between the first and third week.
Client:	Should I bring the baby when it drops off?

421

Pediatra:	Limpie alrededor del cordón umbilical con alcohol.
Cliente:	¿Qué tan frecuentemente?
Pediatrician:	Clean the area around the umbilical cord with alcohol.
Client:	How often?

422

Pediatra:	Venga a verme si se está hinchando o poniéndose rojo.
Cliente:	Bien.
Pediatrician:	Come to see me if it's getting red or swollen.
Client:	O.K.

423

Pediatra:	Es mejor darle pecho a su hijo(a).
Cliente:	¿Por qué razón?
Pediatrician:	It's better to breast feed your child.
Client:	Why?

424

Pediatra:	Es mejor darle pecho a su hijo(a) hasta la edad de 6 meses.
Cliente:	Así lo haré.
Pediatrician:	It's better to breast feed your son(daugther) until he(she) is 6 months old.
Client:	I will do that.

425

Pediatra:	No le dé leche fresca de vaca.
Cliente:	Está bien.
Pediatrician:	Do not give him cow's milk.
Client:	O.K.

426

Pediatra:	No tome medicamentos mientras está dando pecho.
Cliente:	¿De ningún tipo?
Pediatrician:	Don't take medications during breast feeding.
Client:	Of any kind?

427

Pediatra:	La circuncisión previene infecciones.
Cliente:	¿Usted la recomienda?
Pediatrician:	Circumcision prevents infections.
Client:	Do you recommend it?

428

Pediatra:	Escuche con atención a su hijo(a).
Cliente:	Siempre lo hago.
Pediatrician:	Pay attention to what your child is saying.
Client:	I always do.

429

Pediatra:	Hágale saber que entendió lo que dijo.
Cliente:	De acuerdo.
Pediatrician:	Let him (her) know that you understand.
Client:	I agree.

430

Pediatra:	Si está enojada, tómese unos minutos para tranquilizarse.
Cliente:	Eso es lo más difícil para mi.
Pediatrician:	If you are upset allow a few minutes to calm down.
Client:	That is the most difficult thing for me.

431

Pediatra:	Premie la buena conducta.
Cliente:	¿Con regalos o con palabras?
Pediatrician:	Praise good behavior.
Client:	With gifts or with words?

432

Pediatra:	Ignore la mala conducta.
Cliente:	¿Cómo?
Pediatrician:	Ignore bad behavior.
Client:	How?

433

Pediatra:	Hágale saber que lo (la) quiere, pero no aprueba su conducta.
Cliente:	Espero que eso me ayude.
Pediatrician:	Let him (her) know that you love him (her) but not his (her) behavior.
Client:	I hope this will help.

434

Pediatra:	No castigue con golpes.
Cliente:	Nunca lo hago.
Pediatrician:	Don't use corporal punishment.
Client:	I never do.

435

Pediatra:	Déle tiempo para que se calme.
Cliente:	¿Cuánto tiempo es suficiente?
Pediatrician:	Give him (her) time to calm down.
Client:	How much time is enough?

436

Pediatra:	¿Llora mucho el (la) niño(a)?
Cliente:	Sí, por las noches.
Pediatrician:	Does the child cry a lot?
Client:	Yes, during the night.

437

Pediatra:	¿Hace berrinches?
Cliente:	Cuando no consigue lo que quiere.
Pediatrician:	Does he (she) have temper tantrums?
Client:	When he (she) doesn't get what he (she) wants.

438

Pediatra:	Sea tolerante, ofrézcale una alternativa.
Cliente:	¿Qué clase de alternativa?
Pediatrician:	Be tolerant, offer him (her) an alternative.
Client:	What kind of alternative?

439

Pediatra:	Manténgase tranquila.
Cliente:	Eso es difícil.
Pediatrician:	Keep calm.
Client:	That is hard.

440

Pediatra:	Háblele con cariño.
Cliente:	Pero, si todo el tiempo lo hago.
Pediatrician:	Talk to him (her) affectionately.
Client:	But I do that all the time.

441

Pediatra:	Sea firme cuando sea necesario.
Cliente:	Bueno.
Pediatrician:	Be firm when necessary.
Client:	Fine.

442

Pediatra:	No permita que los berrinches la alteren.
Cliente:	Trataré de controlarme.
Pediatrician:	Don't let temper tantrums change you.
Client:	I will try to control myself.

443

Pediatra:	Enséñele a usar el baño.
Cliente:	Ya lo estoy haciendo.
Pediatrician:	Teach him (her) to use the toilet.
Client:	I have started doing so.

444

Pediatra:	No le dé aspirina a su hijo(a).
Cliente:	¿Qué debo darle?
Pediatrician:	Don't give aspirin to your child.
Client:	What should I give him (her) instead?

445

Pediatra:	Llame al (a la) doctor(a) si la temperatura es mayor a 102°.
Cliente:	¿Qué debo hacer mientras?
Pediatrician:	Call the doctor if the temperature goes above 102° F.
Client:	What should I do in the meantime?

446

Pediatra:	Mantenga una rutina de alimentación.
Cliente:	Así lo haré.
Pediatrician:	Keep a feeding routine.
Client:	I will do that.

447

Pediatra:	¿Tiene dificultad para respirar?
Cliente:	Sí, tose mucho.
Pediatrician:	Does he (she) have difficulty breathing?
Client:	Yes, he (she) coughs a lot.

448

Pediatra:	No se impaciente.
Cliente:	Está bien.
Pediatrician:	Don't be impatient.
Client:	Fine.

449

Pediatra:	Cambie los pañales lo más frecuentemente posible.
Cliente:	Está bien.
Pediatrician:	Change the diapers as frequently as possible.
Client:	Fine.

450

Pediatra:	Aplique crema protectora para bebés.
Cliente:	¿Me dará una receta?
Pediatrician:	Apply protective baby cream.
Client:	Will you give me a prescription?

451

Pediatra:	Aplique talco para bebés.
Cliente:	Lo hago siempre que lo cambio de pañal.
Pediatrician:	Apply baby powder.
Client:	I do it every time I change the diapers.

452

Pediatra:	Cambie de detergente.
Cliente:	¿Qué marca me recomienda?
Pediatrician:	Change the detergent.
Client:	What brand do you recommend?

453

Pediatra:	¿Tiene diarrea con frecuencia?
Cliente:	No, sólo durante la última semana.
Pediatrician:	Does he (her) have diarrhea frequently?
Client:	No, only this last week.

454

Pediatra:	Déle líquidos cada vez que obre.
Cliente:	No quiere tomar nada.
Pediatrician:	Give him (her) fluids each time he (she) has a bowel movement.
Client:	He doesn't want to drink anything.

455

Pediatra:	No le dé Pedialyte por más de 24 horas.
Cliente:	¿Qué le doy entonces?
Pediatrician:	Don't give him (her) Pedialyte for more than 24 hours.
Client:	What should I give him (her) instead?

456

Pediatra:	No le dé aspirinas a los niños.
Cliente:	¿Qué les doy entonces?
Pediatrician:	Do not give aspirin to the children.
Client:	What should I give them then?

457

Pediatra:	Evite los alimentos altos en azúcar.
Cliente:	Le fascinan los dulces.
Pediatrician:	Avoid foods high in sugars.
Client:	He (She) loves candy.

458

Pediatra:	¿Hay sangre en el pañal?
Cliente:	No lo he notado.
Pediatrician:	Is there blood in the diaper?
Client:	I have not noticed any.

459

Pediatra:	¿La orina está muy obscura?
Cliente:	No, es normal.
Pediatrician:	Is the urine dark?
Client:	No, it's normal.

460

Pediatra:	¿Hay sangre en el vómito?
Cliente:	No.
Pediatrician:	Is there any blood in the vomit?
Client:	No.

461

Pediatra:	Motive a su niño(a) a tomar más líquidos.
Cliente:	Lo haré más seguido.
Pediatrician:	Encourage your child to take more fluids.
Client:	I will do so more often.

462

Pediatra:	¿Ha tenido convulsiones?
Cliente:	No, pero llora mucho.
Pediatrician:	Has he(she) had any convulsions?
Client:	No, but he(she) cries a lot.

463

Pediatra:	Su hijo(a) necesita una vacuna.
Cliente:	¿Qué vacuna necesita?
Pediatrician:	Your son(daughter) needs a vaccination.
Client:	What vaccination does he(she) need?

464

Pediatra:	¿Han vacunado a su hijo(a)?
Cliente:	Sí, pero no recuerdo de qué.
Pediatrician:	Has your son (daughter) been immunized?
Client:	Yes, but I don't remember for what.

465

Pediatra:	¿Qué vacunas le han puesto?
Cliente:	Polio y difteria solamente.
Pediatrician:	What vaccinations has he (she) received?
Client:	Only polio and diphtheria.

466

Pediatra:	¿Nos autoriza usted que le pongamos la vacuna?
Cliente:	¿Qué vacuna es?
Pediatrician:	Do we have your authorization to give him (her) a vaccination?
Client:	What vaccination is it?

467

Pediatra:	¿Tuvo alguna reacción con la vacuna?
Cliente:	Sí, sólo un poco de calentura, como era esperado.
Pediatrician:	Did he (she) have a reaction to the vaccine?
Client:	Yes, only a slight fever as expected.

468

Pediatra:	Le vamos a hacer una prueba de tuberculosis.
Cliente:	¿Es necesario?
Pediatrician:	We are going to give him (her) a TB test.
Client:	Is it necessary?

469

Pediatra:	La ley exige que su hijo(a) se ponga la vacuna contra la polio.
Cliente:	Creo que ya se la pusieron.
Pediatrician:	The law requires that your son (daugther) get a polio shot.
Client:	I believe he (she) already had it.

470

Pediatra:	La ley requiere que le hagamos la prueba de tuberculosis.
Cliente:	Bueno.
Pediatrician:	The law requires that we give him (her) a TB skin test.
Client:	Fine.

Sexuality and Contraception
Anticonceptivos y sexualidad

471

Médico: ¿Usa usted algún tipo de control de natalidad?

Cliente: No, quiero que me recomiende alguno.

Doctor: Do you use some kind of birth control?

Client: No, would you recommend some for me?

472

Médico: ¿Usa usted anticonceptivos?

Cliente: No, me han dicho que no son buenos.

Doctor: Do you use contraceptives?

Client: No, I've been told they are no good.

473

Médico: ¿Qué clase de prevención para el embarazo utiliza usted?

Cliente: El ritmo.

Doctor: What kind of birth control do you use?

Client: The rhythm method.

474

Médico: Los preservativos también protegen de las enfermedades venéreas.

Cliente: Sí, los uso todo el tiempo.

Doctor: Condoms also protect from venereal diseases.

Client: Yes, I use them all the time.

475

Médico: Ningún método es 100% efectivo.

Cliente: ¿Cuál es el mejor?

Doctor: No method is 100% effective.

Client: Which one is the best?

476

Médico: ¿Le han hecho la vasectomía?

Cliente: No, ¿cuáles son los efectos secundarios?

Doctor: Have you had a vasectomy?

Client: No, what are the side effects?

477

Médico: ¿Quiere que le liguen las trompas?

Cliente: Sí, pero no estoy segura de las consecuencias.

Doctor: Do you want to have a tubal ligation?

Client: Yes, but I'm not sure of the consequences.

478

Médico: ¿Quiere hacerse la vasectomía?

Cliente: No, aún no me decido.

Doctor: Do you want to have a vasectomy?

Client: No, I have not decided yet.

479

Médico: ¿Toma la píldora?

Cliente: La dejé de tomar.

Doctor: Are you taking the pill?

Client: I stopped taking it.

480

Médico: ¿Quiere tomar la píldora?

Cliente: Ya no, prefiero el dispositivo intrauterino.

Doctor: Do you want to take the pill?

Client: Not any more, I would rather have an IUD.

481

Médico: ¿Tiene un aparato intrauterino?

Cliente: Sí, ¿qué otra opción recomienda?

Doctor: Do you have an IUD?

Client: Yes, what other option do you recommend?

482

Médico: ¿Le han diagnosticado alguna enfermedad venérea?

Cliente: Nunca.

Doctor: Have you been diagnosed with a venereal desease?

Client: Never.

483

Médico: ¿Tiene Herpes Genital?

Cliente: No.

Doctor: Do you have Genital Herpes?

Client: No.

484

Médico: ¿Le han diagnosticado SIDA?

Cliente: No. ¿Debo de hacerme la prueba?

Doctor: Have you been diagnosed with AIDS?

Client: No. Should I be tested?

485

Médico: ¿Quiere hacerse la prueba del SIDA?

Cliente: No lo creo necesario, no soy de la población en alto riesgo.

Doctor: Do you want to have an AIDS test?

Client: I don't think it's necessary, I don't belong to the high risk population.

486

Médico: Evite el contacto sexual mientras su pareja esté bajo tratamiento.

Cliente: ¿Por cuánto tiempo será esto?

Doctor: Avoid sexual intercourse while your partner is under treatment.

Client: For how long will this be?

487

Médico: ¿Ha perdido peso repentinamente?

Cliente: No.

Doctor: Have you lost weight suddenly?

Client: No.

488

Médico: ¿Tiene fiebre y suda durante las noches?

Cliente: No me da fiebre, pero sí sudo mucho.

Doctor: Do you have a fever, and sweat at night?

Client: I don't have a fever, but I sweat a lot.

489

Médico: ¿Se siente muy fatigada?

Cliente: De vez en cuando.

Doctor: Do you feel tired?

Client: Once in a while.

490

Médico: ¿Tiene diarrea con frecuencia?

Cliente: No.

Doctor: Do you have diarrhea frequently?

Client: No.

491

Médico: ¿Le salen fuegos?

Cliente: Cuando me pongo al sol, solamente.

Doctor: Do you get cold sores?

Client: Only when I expose myself to the sun.

492

Médico: Evite el contacto sexual sin el uso de condones.

Cliente: Está bien.

Doctor: Avoid sexual contact without condoms.

Client: O.K.

Mental Health / Salud mental

493

Trabajador Social: ¿Ha tenido que ver a un psiquiatra por alguna razón?

Cliente: Toda mi vida.

Social Worker: Have you had to see a psychiatrist for any reason?

Client: All of my life.

494

Trabajador Social: ¿Ha sido usted hospitalizado por razones psiquiátricas?

Cliente: Sí, el mes pasado.

Social Worker: Have you been hospitalized for psychiatric reasons?

Client: Yes, last month.

495

Trabajador Social: ¿Ha recibido servicios de administración de casos?

Cliente: Sí, tengo un trabajador.

Social Worker: Have you received case management services?

Client: Yes, I have a case worker.

496

Trabajador social:	¿Ha estado en alguna crisis que haya requerido ayuda de emergencia?
Cliente:	Por razones físicas solamente.
Social Worker:	Have you been in a crisis that requires an emergency intervention?
Client:	For physical reasons only.

497

Trabajador social:	¿Por qué razón le hospitalizaron?
Cliente:	Me sentía deprimido(a).
Social Worker:	For what reason have you been hospitalized?
Client:	I was feeling depressed.

498

Trabajador social:	¿Algún miembro de su familia ha sufrido de alguna enfermedad mental?
Cliente:	Sí, mi tío.
Social Worker:	Has anybody in your family suffered from a mental illness?
Client:	Yes, my uncle.

499

Trabajador social:	¿Qué medicamentos está tomando ahora?
Cliente:	Haldol y Cogentin.
Social Worker:	What medications are you currently taking?
Client:	Haldol and Cogentin.

500

Trabajador social:	¿Cómo está su salud física?
Cliente:	Bien.
Social Worker:	How is your physical health?
Client:	Fine.

501

Trabajador social:	¿Qué otros medicamentos está tomando?
Cliente:	Aspirina de vez en cuando.
Social Worker:	What other medications are you taking?
Client:	Aspirin once in a while.

502

Trabajador social:	¿Alguien en su familia se ha tratado de suicidar?
Cliente:	Mi abuelita.
Social Worker:	Has anybody in your family tried to commit suicide?
Client:	My grandmother.

503

Trabajador social:	¿Usted ha pensado en suicidarse alguna vez?
Cliente:	Nunca.
Social Worker:	Have you ever thought of committing suicide?
Client:	Never.

504

Trabajador social:	¿En los últimos 30 días usted ha pensado en el suicidio?
Cliente:	Sí, me siento muy deprimido.
Social Worker:	In the last 30 days have you thought of suicide?
Client:	Yes, I feel very depressed.

505

Trabajador social:	¿Tiene algún plan para suicidarse?
Cliente:	Sí, me iba a lanzar desde un edificio.
Social Worker:	Do you have a plan to commit suicide?
Client:	Yes, I was going to throw myself from a building.

506

Trabajador social: ¿Ha tratado de suicidarse alguna vez?
Cliente: Solamente una vez.
Social Worker: Have you ever attempted suicide?
Client: Only once.

507

Trabajador social: ¿Ha asaltado usted a alguna persona?
Cliente: No.
Social Worker: Have you ever assaulted anyone?
Client: No.

508

Trabajador social: ¿Ha amenazado a alguien?
Cliente: Sólo cuando ha sido necesario.
Social Worker: Have you threatened anyone?
Client: Only when necessary.

509

Trabajador social: ¿Ha sido víctima de algún asalto?
Cliente: Sí, en varias ocasiones.
Social Worker: Have you been a victim of an assault?
Client: Yes, on several occasions.

510

Trabajador social: ¿Consume usted algún tipo de droga?
Cliente: No, nunca.
Social Worker: Do you use drugs?
Client: No, never.

511

Trabajador social:	¿Toma usted bebidas alcohólicas?
Cliente:	Ocasionalmente.
Social Worker:	Do you drink alcohol?
Client:	Occasionally.

512

Trabajador social:	¿Cuántos tragos se toma usted diariamente?
Cliente:	Sólo 4 al día.
Social Worker:	How many drinks do you have a day?
Client:	Only 4 a day.

513

Trabajador social:	¿Ha consumido crystal?
Cliente:	Sí, cuando vivía con mi tío.
Social Worker:	Have you taken crystal?
Client:	Yes, when I lived with my uncle.

514

Trabajador social:	¿Ha usado cocaína?
Cliente:	No, nunca.
Social Worker:	Have you done cocaine?
Client:	No, never.

515

Trabajador social:	¿Ha fumado crack?
Cliente:	No, nunca.
Social Worker:	Have you smoked crack?
Client:	No, never.

516

Trabajador social:	¿Ha tomado LSD?
Cliente:	No, nunca he tomado drogas.
Social Worker:	Have you taken LSD?
Client:	No, I have never taken any drugs.

517

Trabajador social:	¿Ha fumado mariguana?
Cliente:	Nunca.
Social Worker:	Have you smoked marijuana?
Client:	Never.

518

Trabajador social:	¿Ha usado heroína?
Cliente:	No.
Social Worker:	Have you used heroin?
Client:	No.

519

Trabajador social:	¿Está usted en algún programa de desintoxicación?
Cliente:	Sí, en el hospital Mercy.
Social Worker:	Are you enrolled in a detox program?
Client:	Yes, in Mercy hospital.

520

Trabajador social:	¿Desea usted dejar de usar drogas?
Cliente:	Sí, ¿dónde puedo recibir tratamiento?
Social Worker:	Do you want to stop using drugs?
Client:	Yes, where can I get treatment?

521

Trabajador social:	¿Quiere usted participar en un programa de Alcohólicos Anónimos?
Cliente:	Sí ¿tiene usted alguna información?
Social Worker:	Do you want to join an AA program?
Client:	Yes, do you have any information?

522

Trabajador social:	¿Cuándo fue la última vez que utilizó alguna droga?
Cliente:	Hace varios años.
Social Worker:	When was the last time you used drugs?
Client:	Several years ago.

523

Trabajador social:	¿Consumió alguna droga durante la semana pasada?
Cliente:	Sí, el viernes pasado.
Social Worker:	Have you taken any drugs during the past week?
Client:	Yes, last Friday.

524

Trabajador social:	¿Toma usted drogas por lo menos una vez al mes?
Cliente:	De ninguna manera, nunca las he usado.
Social Worker:	Do you take drugs at least once a month?
Client:	Under no circumstances, I have never used them.

525

Trabajador social:	¿Toma usted alguna droga más de una vez al día?
Cliente:	Fumo cigarrillos, nada más.
Social Worker:	Do you take any drugs more than once a day?
Client:	I only smoke cigarettes.

526

Trabajador social:	¿Fuma usted?
Cliente:	Sí, pero muy poco.
Social Worker:	Do you smoke?
Client:	Yes, but very little.

527

Trabajador social:	¿Cuántos cigarrillos al día?
Cliente:	Entre 4 y 8.
Social Worker:	How many cigarettes do you smoke a day?
Client:	Between 4 and 8.

528

Trabajador social:	¿Toma café?
Cliente:	Varias tazas al día.
Social Worker:	Do you drink coffee?
Client:	Several cups a day.

529

Trabajador social:	¿Cuántas tasas de café toma al día?
Cliente:	No más de 3.
Social Worker:	How many cups of coffee do you drink a day?
Client:	No more than 3.

530

Trabajador social:	¿Se siente triste?
Cliente:	Sólo cuando tengo problemas.
Social Worker:	Do you feel sad?
Client:	Only when I have problems.

531

Trabajador social:	¿Está preocupado?
Cliente:	Un poco.
Social Worker:	Are you worried?
Client:	A little bit.

532

Trabajador social:	¿Se siente agitado?
Cliente:	Sí, estoy enojado.
Social Worker:	Do you feel agitated?
Client:	Yes, I'm angry.

533

Trabajador social:	¿Se siente culpable?
Cliente:	No tengo de qué.
Social Worker:	Do you feel guilty?
Client:	I don't have a reason to.

534

Trabajador social:	¿Se siente irritado?
Cliente:	Sólo cuando me hacen enojar.
Social Worker:	Do you feel irritated?
Client:	Only when somebody makes me mad.

535

Trabajador social:	¿Se siente impulsivo?
Cliente:	¿Qué quiere decir con eso?
Social Worker:	Do you feel impulsive?
Client:	What do you mean by that?

536

Trabajador social:	¿Tiene miedo?
Cliente:	Sí, por las noches.
Social Worker:	Are you afraid?
Client:	Yes, at night.

537

Trabajador social:	¿Se siente raro?
Cliente:	Sí, como si alguien me tocara.
Social Worker:	Do you feel strange?
Client:	Yes, like someone is touching me.

538

Trabajador social:	¿Siente que alguien le está siguiendo?
Cliente:	Sí, constantemente en las calles.
Social Worker:	Do you feel like someone is following you?
Client:	Yes, constantly on the streets.

539

Trabajador social:	¿Ha pensado alguna vez en irse?
Cliente:	Sí, ya no tolero esta situación.
Social Worker:	Have you ever thought of running away?
Client:	Yes, I can't stand this situation any longer.

540

Trabajador social:	¿Creé que tiene alguna enfermedad que los doctores no encuentran?
Cliente:	Sí, es que no me han diagnosticado bien.
Social Worker:	Do you belive you have an illness that the doctors have not detected?
Client:	Yes, it's because they haven't diagnosed me correctly.

541

Trabajador social:	¿Ha perdido las esperanzas?
Cliente:	Sí, me siento deprimido(a).
Social Worker:	Have you lost hope?
Client:	Yes, I feel depressed.

542

Trabajador social:	¿Es usted una persona religiosa?
Cliente:	Sí, voy a misa todos los domingos.
Social Worker:	Are you a religious person?
Client:	Yes, I go to church every Sunday.

543

Trabajador social:	¿Le preocupa el sexo?
Cliente:	¿De qué manera?
Social Worker:	Are you preoccupied with sex?
Client:	In what way?

544

Trabajador social:	¿Siente que los demás son culpables de sus problemas?
Cliente:	Sí.
Social Worker:	Do you feel others are to blame for your problems?
Client:	Yes.

545

Trabajador social:	¿Escucha voces?
Cliente:	Sí, me atormentan constantemente.
Social Worker:	Do you hear voices?
Client:	Yes, they torment me constantly.

546

Trabajador social:	¿Ve cosas que después se da cuenta que no existen?
Cliente:	Sí, veo sombras en la noche.
Social Worker:	Do you see things that later you find aren't there?
Client:	Yes, I see shadows at night.

547

Trabajador social:	¿Siente que alguien lo toca?
Cliente:	Sí, en la espalda.
Social Worker:	Do you feel someone touching you?
Client:	Yes, on my back.

548

Trabajador social:	¿Alguien lo controla?
Cliente:	Sí, son seres de otro planeta.
Social Worker:	Does someone control you?
Client:	Yes, they are beings from other planets.

549

Trabajador social:	¿Usted es una persona muy importante?
Cliente:	Sí, pero nadie me cree.
Social Worker:	Are you an important person?
Client:	Yes, but nobody believes me.

550

Trabajador social:	¿Su esposa le está engañando?
Cliente:	Sí, con el vecino.
Social Worker:	Is your wife cheating on you?
Client:	Yes, with my neighbor.

551

Trabajador social:	¿Sabe qué día es hoy?
Cliente:	No. ¿Qué día es?
Social Worker:	Do you know what day it is?
Client:	No. What day is it?

552

Trabajador social:	¿En dónde estamos?
Cliente:	En un hospital.
Social Worker:	Where are we?
Client:	In a hospital.

553

Trabajador social:	¿Escucha pasos?
Cliente:	Sí, como que alguien viene hacia acá.
Social Worker:	Do you hear footsteps?
Client:	Yes, as if someone is coming this way.

554

Trabajador social:	¿Quién soy yo?
Cliente:	Usted es un médico.
Social Worker:	Who am I?
Client:	You are a doctor.

555

Trabajador social:	¿Le cuesta trabajo concentrarse?
Cliente:	Sí, me siento muy inquieto.
Social Worker:	Is it hard to concentrate?
Client:	Yes, I feel very restless.

556

Trabajador social:	¿Se le olvidan las cosas con frecuencia?
Cliente:	Sí, se me pierden las cosas.
Social Worker:	Do you forget things easily?
Client:	Yes, I lose things.

557

Trabajador social:	¿Necesita ropa?
Cliente:	Sí, no tengo nada qué ponerme.
Social Worker:	Do you need any clothing?
Client:	Yes, I don't have anything to wear.

558

Trabajador social:	¿Necesita comida?
Cliente:	Sí, para mí y para mi familia.
Social Worker:	Do you need food?
Client:	Yes, for me and my family.

559

Trabajador social:	¿Necesita atención médica de emergencia?
Cliente:	Sí, me estoy sintiendo muy mal.
Social Worker:	Do you need emergency medical attention?
Client:	Yes, I'm not feeling well.

560

Trabajador social:	¿Necesita dinero?
Cliente:	Sí, necesito ayuda.
Social Worker:	Do you need money?
Client:	Yes, I need help.

561

Trabajador social:	¿Quiere capacitación profesional?
Cliente:	Sí, quiero trabajar.
Social Worker:	Do you need vocational training?
Client:	Yes, I want to work.

562

Trabajador social:	¿Necesita medicamentos?
Cliente:	Sí, se me terminaron.
Social Worker:	Do you need medications?
Client:	Yes, I ran out.

563

Trabajador social:	¿Vive en la calle?
Cliente:	Sí, cerca de la iglesia.
Social Worker:	Do you live on the street?
Client:	Yes, near the church.

564

Trabajador social:	¿Vive en una casa de asistencia?
Cliente:	Sí, con otras personas.
Social Worker:	Do you live in a board and care home?
Client:	Yes, I live with other people.

565

Trabajador social:	¿Vive en un refugio temporal?
Cliente:	Sí, en el refugio de la catedral.
Social Worker:	Do you live in a shelter?
Client:	Yes, In the Cathedral Shelter.

566

Trabajador social: ¿Cuánto tiempo tiene viviendo ahí?

Cliente: 2 años.

Social Worker: How long have you lived there?

Client: 2 years.

567

Trabajador social: ¿Visita a sus familiares?

Cliente: Muy seguido.

Social Worker: Do you visit your relatives?

Client: Very often.

568

Trabajador social: ¿Visita a sus amigos(as)?

Cliente: Casi nunca.

Social Worker: Do you visit your friends?

Client: Hardly ever.

569

Trabajador social: ¿Asiste a terapia de grupo?

Cliente: Todas las mañanas.

Social Worker: Do you go to group therapy?

Client: Every morning.

570

Trabajador social: ¿Sale con amigos?

Cliente: Sí, voy al cine.

Social Worker: Do you go out with friends?

Client: Yes, I go to the movies.

571

Trabajador social: ¿Cuántas veces come usted al día?

Cliente: Dos solamente.

Social Worker: How many meals a day do you have?

Client: Only two.

572

Trabajador social: ¿Tiene algún problema para llegar a tiempo a sus citas?

Cliente: Sí, no puedo usar el transporte público.

Social Worker: Do you find it difficult getting to your appointments on time?

Client: Yes, I can't use public transportation.

573

Trabajador social: ¿Sabe usar el teléfono?

Cliente: No, no le entiendo a la operadora.

Social Worker: Do you know how to use the telephone?

Client: No, I don't understand the operator.

574

Trabajador social: ¿Sabe utilizar el transporte público?

Cliente: Sí, voy a todas partes en él.

Social Worker: Do you know how to use public transportation?

Client: Yes, I go everywhere on it.

575

Trabajador social: ¿Está en algún programa de entrenamiento?

Cliente: Sí, para minusválidos.

Social Worker: Are you in a training program?

Client: Yes, for the handicapped.

576

Trabajador social:	¿En qué programa de entrenamiento está?
Cliente:	En el de la clínica.
Social Worker:	In what program are you?
Client:	The one in the clinic.

577

Trabajador social:	¿Hace algún trabajo voluntario?
Cliente:	Sí, ayudo en la biblioteca.
Social Worker:	Do you do any volunteer work?
Client:	Yes, I help in the library.

578

Trabajador social:	¿Toma las medicinas tal como se las prescribieron?
Cliente:	No, no le entiendo a las instrucciones.
Social Worker:	Do you take your medications as prescribed?
Client:	No, I don't understand the instructions.

579

Trabajador social:	¿Cuándo fue su última visita con el (la) dentista?
Cliente:	Hace como un año.
Social Worker:	When was your last visit with the dentist?
Client:	About a year ago.

580

Trabajador social:	¿Cuándo fue su última visita con el (la) doctor(a)?
Cliente:	La semana pasada.
Social Worker:	When was your last visit with the doctor?
Client:	Last week.

581

Trabajador social:	¿Cuándo fue su última visita al psiquiatra?
Cliente:	Hace un mes.
Social Worker:	When was your last visit to the psychiatrist?
Client:	A month ago.

582

Trabajador social:	¿Cuánto dinero recibe de AFDC?
Cliente:	No recibo nada todavía.
Social Worker:	How much money do you get from AFDC?
Client:	I don't receive any yet.

583

Trabajador social:	¿Cuánto gana?
Cliente:	Me pagan 4.50 dólares la hora.
Social Worker:	How much do you earn?
Client:	I get paid $4.50 an hour.

584

Trabajador social:	¿Cuánto dinero recibe de GR?
Cliente:	260 dólares mensuales.
Social Worker:	How much money do you get from GR?
Client:	$260 a month.

585

Trabajador social:	¿Cuánto dinero recibe de su retiro?
Cliente:	Solamente 300 dólares mensuales.
Social Worker:	How much money do you get from your retirement?
Client:	Only $300 a month.

586

Trabajador social:	¿Cuánto dinero recibe de SSI?
Cliente:	No sé, tengo un albacea.
Social Worker:	How much money do you get from SSI?
Client:	I don't know, I have a payee.

587

Trabajador social:	¿Cuánto dinero recibe de desempleo?
Cliente:	Recibo 650 dólares al mes.
Social Worker:	How much money do you get from unemployment?
Client:	I get $650 a month.

588

Trabajador social:	¿Tiene un administrador de casos?
Cliente:	Sí, pero no sé cómo se llama.
Social Worker:	Do you have a case manager?
Client:	Yes, but I don't know his (her) name.

589

Trabajador social:	¿Tiene un oficial de libertad condicional?
Cliente:	Sí, me lo asignaron en la corte.
Social Worker:	Do you have a probation officer?
Client:	Yes, he (she) was assigned by the court.

590

Trabajador social:	¿Lo han arrestado por alguna razón?
Cliente:	Sí, por un robo.
Social Worker:	Have you been arrested for any reason?
Client:	Yes, for robbery.

591

Trabajador social:	¿Lo han sentenciado por algún crimen?
Cliente:	No, nunca.
Social Worker:	Have you ever been convicted of a crime?
Client:	No, never.

592

Trabajador social:	¿Se ha escapado de su casa?
Cliente:	Sí, cuando era niño.
Social Worker:	Have you ever run away?
Client:	I ran away from home when I was kid.

593

Trabajador social:	¿Se ha metido en problemas por causa de su conducta sexual?
Cliente:	No, nunca he tenido un problema por eso.
Social Worker:	Have you ever gotten into trouble because of your sexual behavior?
Client:	No, I have never had a problem like that.

594

Trabajador social:	¿Ha destruido alguna cosa cuando está enojado?
Cliente:	Sí, he roto los platos.
Social Worker:	Have you destroyed something when you are upset?
Client:	Yes, I have broken dishes.

595

Trabajador social:	¿Has provocado algún incendio sólo por el gusto de quemar algo?
Cliente:	No, no me gusta el fuego.
Social Worker:	Have you caused a fire just for the pleasure of it?
Client:	No. I don't like fire.

CHAPTER 18 / CAPÍTULO 18

At the Dentist / Con el dentista

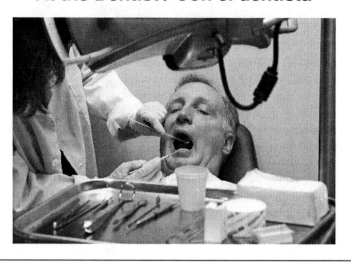

596

Recepcionista:	Buenas tardes.
Cliente:	Buenas tardes. ¿Es el consultorio dental del Dr. Fernández?
Receptionist:	Good afternoon.
Client:	Good afternoon. Is this Dr. Fernandez dental office?

597

Recepcionista:	¿Cómo le puedo ayudar?
Cliente:	Necesito ver al doctor.
Receptionist:	How can we help you?
Client:	I need to see the Doctor.

598

Recepcionista:	¿Es una emergencia?
Cliente:	No, pero tengo un dolor.
Receptionist:	Is this an emergency?
Client:	No, but I have a pain.

599

Recepcionista:	¿Tiene dolor en la muela?
Cliente:	Sí, muy fuerte.
Receptionist:	Do you have a toothache?
Client:	Yes, very severe.

600

Recepcionista:	¿Viene a examen y limpieza?
Cliente:	Sí, solamente para examen y limpieza.
Receptionist:	Are you here for an examination and a cleaning?
Client:	Yes, only for examination and a cleaning.

601

Recepcionista:	¿Es su primera visita con nosotros?
Cliente:	No, es la segunda visita.
Receptionist:	Is this your first time in our office?
Client:	No, it's my second one.

602

Recepcionista:	¿Cómo supo de nosotros?
Cliente:	Mi cuñada me lo recomendó.
Receptionist:	How did you hear about us?
Client:	My sister in law recommended you.

603

Recepcionista:	¿Cómo se llama usted?
Cliente:	Arturo Jiménez.
Receptionist:	What is your name?
Client:	Arturo Jimenez.

604

Recepcionista:	¿Cuál es su número de teléfono?
Cliente:	Mi teléfono es 123-0987.
Receptionist:	What is your telephone number?
Client:	My phone number is 123-0987.

605

Recepcionista:	¿Cuál es su dirección?
Cliente:	465 Camino del Cerro Rojo.
Receptionist:	What is your address?
Client:	465 Camino del Cerro Rojo.

606

Recepcionista:	¿Cuántos años tiene?
Cliente:	Tengo 32 años de edad.
Receptionist:	How old are you?
Client:	I'm 32 years old.

607

Recepcionista:	¿Cuántos años tiene el paciente?
Cliente:	12 años.
Receptionist:	How old is the patient?
Client:	12 years old.

608

Recepcionista:	Si el paciente es menor de 18 años, se requiere que un adulto responsable esté presente.
Cliente:	Su hermana mayor estará con él.
Receptionist:	If the patient is less than 18 years old a parent or a guardian must be present.
Client:	His older sister will be with him.

609

Recepcionista: Traiga una lista de las medicinas que está tomando.

Cliente: Está bien.

Receptionist: Bring a list of the medications you are taking.

Client: Fine.

610

Recepcionista: ¿Tiene usted seguro dental?

Cliente: Sí, aquí está.

Receptionist: Do you have dental insurance?

Client: Yes, here it is.

611

Recepcionista: ¿Cuál es el nombre de su compañía de seguro?

Cliente: Dental Plus.

Receptionist: What is the name of the insurance carrier?

Client: Dental Plus.

612

Recepcionista: ¿Cuántos seguros dentales tiene?

Cliente: Uno solamente.

Receptionist: How many dental insurances do you have?

Client: Only one.

613

Recepcionista: ¿Tiene tarjeta de su compañía de seguros?

Cliente: Sí, pero no la traigo conmigo

Receptionist: Do you have an insurance ID card?

Client: Yes, but I don't have it with me.

614

Recepcionista:	¿Está el seguro a su nombre?
Cliente:	No, está a nombre de mi esposa.
Receptionist:	Is the insurance in your name?
Client:	No, it's in my wife's name.

615

Recepcionista:	¿Tiene usted cobertura bajo la póliza de un miembro de su familia?
Cliente:	Sí, la de mi esposa(o).
Receptionist:	Are you covered by a family member's dental insurance?
Client:	Yes, my wife's.

616

Recepcionista:	¿Cuál es el número de registro de su aseguradora?
Cliente:	El número es, 10293847.
Receptionist:	What is the insurance registration number?
Client:	The number is 10293847.

617

Recepcionista:	¿Está vigente su cobertura?
Cliente:	Sí, vence hasta el 98.
Receptionist:	Is your insurance coverage current?
Client:	Yes, it expires in 1998.

618

Recepcionista:	¿Cuándo quiere venir?
Cliente:	Pasado mañana, si es posible.
Receptionist:	When would you like to come in?
Client:	The day after tomorrow, if possible.

619

Recepcionista: La próxima cita disponible es el lunes.

Cliente: El lunes me es imposible.

Receptionist: The next available appointment is on Monday.

Client: Monday is impossible for me.

620

Recepcionista: Por favor traiga la documentación de su seguro.

Cliente: ¿Con la credencial basta?

Receptionist: Please bring your insurance documentation.

Client: Is the card enough?

621

Recepcionista: Por favor traiga una forma de pago en caso de que halla cargos.

Cliente: Sí.

Receptionist: Please bring a payment form in case any charges occur?

Client: Yes.

622

Recepcionista: Si necesita cancelar, hágalo 24 horas antes de su cita.

Cliente: ¿A qué número debo de hablar?

Receptionist: If you need to cancel you must call 24 hours prior to your appointment.

Client: What number should I call?

623

Recepcionista: Hay un cargo de 25 dólares si no se presenta a la cita.

Cliente: Aquí estaré.

Receptionist: There is a $ 25.00 charge if you fail to keep your appointment.

Client: I will be there.

624

Recepcionista:	Gracias por hablar, lo veremos pronto.
Cliente:	Gracias a usted.
Receptionist:	Thank you for calling, we will see you soon.
Client:	Thank you.

625

Recepcionista:	Por favor hable si tiene alguna otra pregunta.
Cliente:	Muchas gracias.
Receptionist:	Please call if you have any more questions.
Client:	Thank you.

626

Recepcionista:	Por favor firme la forma de registro.
Cliente:	No tengo pluma.
Receptionist:	Please sign your name on the registration form.
Client:	I don't have a pen.

627

Recepcionista:	Usted necesita llenar y firmar estas formas.
Cliente:	Ya las llené la semana pasada.
Receptionist:	You need to fill out and sign these forms.
Client:	I filled them out last week.

628

Recepcionista:	Por favor tome asiento.
Cliente:	Gracias señorita.
Receptionist:	Please take a seat.
Client:	Thank you.

629

Recepcionista: Le llamaremos cuando sea su turno.

Cliente: ¿Tardará mucho?

Receptionist: We will call you when your turn comes.

Client: Will it take long?

630

Recepcionista: Sr. (Sra.) Domínguez el doctor lo(a) verá ahora.

Cliente: Voy.

Receptionist: Mr. (Mrs.) Dominguez the Dr. will see you know.

Client: Coming.

631

Recepcionista: El costo de su visita de hoy será de 35 dólares.

Cliente: ¿Puedo pagar con un cheque?

Receptionist: Your fee for today's visit will be $35.00.

Client: Can I pay with a check?

632

Recepcionista: El doctor quiere verlo(a) otra vez en dos semanas.

Cliente: Estaré fuera de la ciudad.

Receptionist: The doctor wants to see you again in two weeks.

Client: I will be out of town.

633

Recepcionista: ¿Quiere hacer una cita?

Cliente: Sí, por favor.

Receptionist: Would you like to schedule an appointment?

Client: Yes, please.

634

Recepcionista: Su próxima cita va a tardar una hora.

Cliente: ¿Por qué tanto?

Receptionist: Your next appointment should take about one hour.

Client: Why so long?

635

Recepcionista: No olvide tomar su medicina.

Cliente: Claro que no.

Receptionist: Don't forget to take your medications.

Client: Of course not.

636

Recepcionista: Gracias por su visita.

Cliente: De nada.

Receptionist: Thank you for visiting us today.

Client: Your welcome.

637

Asistente dental: Hola mi nombre es Esperanza Buenrostro.

Cliente: Mucho gusto.

Dental Assistant: Hello my name is Esperanza Buenrostro.

Client: Glad to meet you

638

Asistente dental: ¿Es su primera visita con nosotros?

Cliente: Sí, la primera.

Dental Assistant: Is this your first time in our office?

Client: Yes, the first time.

639

Asistente dental: Usted verá al doctor García.

Cliente: De acuerdo.

Dental Assistant: You will be seeing Dr. Garcia today.

Client: OK.

640

Asistente dental: ¿Tiene usted un dolor de muelas.?

Cliente: Sí, punzadas muy fuertes.

Dental Assistant: Do you have a toothache?

Client: Yes, very sharp pains.

641

Asistente dental: ¿Puede señalarme el diente que le molesta?

Cliente: Sí, éste.

Dental Assistant: Can you point to the tooth that is hurting you?

Client: Yes, this one.

642

Asistente dental: ¿Por cuánto tiempo le ha estado doliendo?

Cliente: Por una semana.

Dental Assistant: How long has the tooth been hurting you?

Client: For a week.

643

Asistente dental: ¿Qué clase de dolor es?

Cliente: Un dolor agudo.

Dental Assistant: What kind of pain is it?

Client: A sharp pain.

644

Asistente dental: ¿Es un dolor punzante o profundo?

Cliente: Profundo.

Dental Assistant: Is it a sharp or deep pain?

Client: Deep.

645

Asistente dental: ¿Está usted tomando alguna medicina?

Cliente: No, ninguna.

Dental Assistant: Are you taking any medications?

Client: No, none.

646

Asistente dental: ¿Leyó y contestó el cuestionario?

Cliente: Sí, respondí a todas las preguntas.

Dental Assistant: Did you read and fill out the health questionnaire?

Client: Yes, I answered all of the questions.

647

Asistente dental: ¿Le sangran las encías cuando se lava los dientes?

Cliente: Sí, siempre.

Dental Assistant: Do your gums bleed when you brush?

Client: Yes, always.

648

Asistente dental: ¿Están sus dientes sensibles al calor y al frío.

Cliente: Sí, especialmente al frío.

Dental Assistant: Are your teeth sensitive to hot or cold?

Client: Yes, especially cold.

649

Asistente dental: ¿Está usted embarazada?
Cliente: No.
Dental Assistant: Are you pregnant?
Client: No.

650

Asistente dental: ¿Cuántos meses tiene de embarazo?
Cliente: Tengo 5 meses.
Dental Assistant: How many months pregnant are you?
Client: I'm 5 months pregnant.

651

Asistente dental: Necesito tomar una radiografía de ese diente.
Cliente: Está bien.
Dental Assistant: I need to take an X-ray of that tooth.
Client: Fine.

652

Asistente dental: Requerimos de una serie de radiografías para hacer un examen completo.
Cliente: Bueno.
Dental Assistant: We need a series of X-rays for a complete examination.
Client: Fine.

653

Asistente dental: Tengo que ponerle una protección contra los Rayos - X.
Cliente: Está bien.
Dental Assistant: I must place a shield on you for X-ray protection.
Client: OK.

654

Asistente dental: Detenga la radiografía con su dedo así.

Cliente: ¿Así está bien?

Dental Assistant: Hold the X-ray with your finger like this.

Client: Is this OK?

655

Asistente dental: Muerda con cuidado la pieza que sostiene la radiografía.

Cliente: ¿Por cuánto tiempo?

Dental Assistant: Bite down gently on the X-ray holder.

Client: For how long?

656

Asistente dental: No se mueva.

Cliente: Está bien.

Dental Assistant: Don't move.

Client: Fine.

657

Asistente dental: Necesitamos una radiografía más.

Cliente: Bueno.

Dental Assistant: We need one more X-ray.

Client: Fine.

658

Asistente dental: El doctor estará con usted pronto.

Cliente: Gracias.

Dental Assistant: The Doctor will be with you shortly.

Client: Thank you.

659

Asistente dental: Voy a tomar una impresión de sus dientes de arriba y de abajo.
Cliente: ¿Es necesario?
Dental Assistant: I am going to take an impression of your upper and lower teeth.
Client: Is it necessary?

660

Asistente dental: Es todo por hoy.
Cliente: ¿Cuándo será la próxima cita?
Dental Assistant: You are all done for today.
Client: When is my next appointment?

661

Asistente dental: Lo (La) acompaño a la recepción.
Cliente: Gracias.
Dental Assistant: I will walk you to reception.
Client: Thank you.

662

Asistente dental: Mucho gusto de conocerlo(a).
Cliente: Igualmente.
Dental Assistant: It was nice meeting you.
Client: Same here.

663

Dentista: Hola soy la (el) doctora(or) Villanueva.
Cliente: Mucho gusto.
Dentist: Hello I am Dr.Villanueva.
Client: I'm very glad.

664

Dentista:	Usted tiene una carie.
Cliente:	¿Sólo una?
Dentist:	You have a cavity.
Client:	Only one?

665

Dentista:	Usted tiene un absceso
Cliente:	¿Me dará antibióticos?
Dentist:	You have an abscess.
Client:	Will you give me antibiotics?

666

Dentista:	Usted tiene un diente roto.
Cliente:	¿Es irreparable?
Dentist:	You have a broken tooth.
Client:	Is it irreparable?

667

Dentista:	Usted tiene gingivitis.
Cliente:	¿Qué debo de hacer para eliminarla?
Dentist:	You have gingivitis.
Client:	What should I do to eliminate it?

668

Dentista:	Usted tiene una enfermedad en las encías, llamada periodontitis.
Cliente:	¿Qué es eso?
Dentist:	You have gum disease called periodontitis.
Client:	What is that?

669

Dentista:	Usted necesita ver a un especialista.
Cliente:	¿Me recomendará uno?
Dentist:	You need to see a specialist.
Client:	Will you recommend one?

670

Dentista:	Usted necesita una limpieza.
Cliente:	¿Qué tan frecuente debo de hacérmela?
Dentist:	Your teeth need cleaning.
Client:	How frequently should I do it?

671

Dentista:	Le vamos a tapar una muela.
Cliente:	¿Me va a doler?
Dentist:	We are going to do a filling.
Client:	Is it going to hurt?

672

Dentista:	Usted requiere de una endodoncia.
Cliente:	Está bien.
Dentist:	You require a root canal.
Client:	Fine.

673

Dentista:	Le vamos a poner un puente.
Cliente:	¿Es necesario?
Dentist:	We are going to put in a bridge.
Client:	Is it necessary?

674

Dentista:	Usted necesita una corona.
Cliente:	Muy bien doctora.
Dentist:	You need a crown.
Client:	Fine Doctor.

675

Dentista:	Le haremos una extracción.
Cliente:	¿Me pondrá un anestésico?
Dentist:	We are going to do an extraction.
Client:	Are you going to give me an anesthetic?

676

Dentista:	Usted requiere de una cirugía.
Cliente:	¿Por qué?
Dentist:	You require surgery.
Client:	Why?

677

Dentista:	Le voy a dar una receta para el dolor.
Cliente:	Sí, tengo mucho dolor.
Dentist:	I am going to give you a prescription for pain.
Client:	Yes, I have a lot of pain.

678

Dentista:	¿Es alérgico a alguna medicina?
Cliente:	Sí, a los antibióticos.
Dentist:	Are you allergic to any medications?
Client:	Yes, to antibiotics.

679

Dentista: Si le salen granos o urticaria deje de tomar las medicinas y hábleme.

Cliente: Lo haré.

Dentist: If you develop a rash or hives stop the medication and call me.

Client: I will.

680

Dentista: Llámeme en caso de emergencia.

Cliente: ¿A qué número?

Dentist: Call me in case of an emergency.

Client: At what number?

681

Dentista: Ya hemos terminado por hoy.

Cliente: Qué bueno.

Dentist: You are all done for today.

Client: Good.

Vocabulario / Vocabulary

Español / Spanish	Inglés / English
Abdomen (el) (n.)	*Belly*
Aborto (el) (n.)	*Abortion*
Absceso (el) (n.)	*Abscess*
Abstinencia (la) (n.)	*Abstinence*
Abuela (la) (n.)	*Grandmother*
Abuelo (el) (n.)	*Grandfather*
Abuso (el) (n.)	*Abuse*
Abuso sexual (el) (n.)	*Sexual abuse*
Accidente (el) (n.)	*Accident*
Aceite (el) (n.)	*Oil*
Ácido (el) (n.)	*Acid*
Ácido úrico (el) (n.)	*Uric acid*
Acné (el) (n.)	*Acne*
Aconsejar (v.)	*Advise*
Acostado, a (adj.)	*Lying down*
Acto sexual (el) (n.)	*Intercourse*
Actualmente (adv.)	*Currently*
Adelgazar (v.)	*Lose weight*
Además (adv.)	*Besides*
Adenoides (la) (n.)	*Adenoids*
Adentro (adv.)	*Inside*
Adicción (la) (n.)	*Addiction*
Administración oral (la) (n.)	*By mouth*
Admisión (la) (n.)	*Admission*
Adrenalina (la) (n.)	*Adrenaline*
Adultos, as (n.)	*Adults*
Advertencia (la) (n.)	*Warning*
Aeróbico (el) (n.)	*Aerobic*
Afectar (v.)	*Affect*
Afectivo, a (adj.)	*Affective*

Agotado, a (adj.)	*Exhausted*
Agrura (la) (n.)	*Heartburn*
Agua (el) (n.)	*Water*
Aguantar (v.)	*Stand*
Agudo, a (adj.)	*Sharp*
Aguja (la) (n.)	*Needle*
Agujero (el) (n.)	*Hole*
Ahora (adv.)	*Now*
Aire (el) (n.)	*Air*
Albúmina (la) (n.)	*Albumin*
Alcohol (el) (n.)	*Alcohol*
Alcohólico, a (n.) (adj.)	*Alcoholic*
Alcoholismo (el) (n.)	*Alcoholism*
Alergia (la) (n.)	*Allergy*
Alérgico, a (adj.)	*Allergic*
Algo (pron.)	*Something*
Algunas veces (adj.)	*Sometimes*
Algunos, as (adj.)	*Some*
Aliento (el) (n.)	*Breath*
Alimento (el) (n.)	*Nourishment*
Aliviar (v.)	*Alleviate*
Alivio (el) (n.)	*Relief*
Almohada (la) (n.)	*Pillow*
Almorzar (v.)	*Lunch*
Alrededor (adv.)	*Around*
Alto, a (adj.)	*High*
Alucinación (la) (n.)	*Hallucination*
Alvéolo (el) (n.)	*Alveoli*
Amable (adj.)	*Polite*
Amarillento, a (adj.)	*Yellowish*
Amarrar (v.)	*Tie*
Ambulancia (la) (n.)	*Ambulance*
Ambulatorio (el) (n.) (adj.)	*Ambulatory*
Amígdala (la) (n.)	*Tonsil*

Amigdalitis (la) (n.)	*Tonsillitis*
Aminoácidos (los) (n.)	*Amino acids*
Amnesia (la) (n.)	*Amnesia*
Ampolla (la) (n.)	*Blister*
Amputación (la) (n.)	*Amputation*
Amputar (v.)	*Amputate*
Anciana (la) (n.)	*Elderly woman*
Anciano (el) (n.)	*Elderly man*
Anemia (la) (n.)	*Anemia*
Anémico, a (adj.)	*Anemic*
Anestesia (la) (n.)	*Anesthesia*
Anfetaminas (las) (n.)	*Amphetamines*
Angina (la) (n.)	*Tonsil*
Ano (el) (n.)	*Anus*
Anorexia (la) (n.)	*Anorexia*
Anormal (adj.)	*Abnormal*
Ansiedad (la) (n.)	*Anxiety*
Anteojos (los) (n.)	*Glasses*
Antiácido (el) (n.) (adj.)	*Antacid*
Antibiótico (el) (n.) (adj.)	*Antibiotic*
Anticonceptivo (el) (n.) (adj.)	*Contraceptive*
Antídoto (el) (n.)	*Antidote*
Antiestamínico (el) (n.) (adj.)	*Antihistamine*
Antiinflamatorio (el) (n.) (adj.)	*Antinflammatory*
Antioxidante (n.) (adj.)	*Antioxidants*
Aorta (la) (n.)	*Aorta*
Apellido (el) (n.)	*Last name*
Apenas (adv.)	*Barely*
Apéndice (el) (n.)	*Appendix*
Apendicitis (la) (n.)	*Appendicitis*
Apetito (el) (n.)	*Appetite*
Apretar (v.)	*Squeeze*
Archivo (el) (n.)	*File*
Ardor (el) (n.)	*Burning*

Arritmia (la) (n.)	*Arrhythmia*
Arteria (la) (n.)	*Artery*
Arteriosclerosis (la) (n.)	*Arteriosclerosis*
Articulación (la) (n.)	*Joint*
Artificial (adj.)	*Artificial*
Artritis (la) (n.)	*Arthritis*
Asfixia (la) (n.)	*Asphyxia*
Asma (el) (n.)	*Asthma*
Asmático, a (adj.)	*Asthmatic*
Aspirina (la) (n.)	*Aspirin*
Astigmatismo (el) (n.)	*Astigmatism*
Asustarse (v. r.)	*Scared*
Ataque (el) (n.)	*Seizure*
Atragantarse (v. r.)	*Choke*
Atrofia (la) (n.)	*Atrophy*
Audífono (el) (n.)	*Hearing aid*
Aumentar (v.)	*Increase*
Auto examen (el) (n.)	*Self exam*
Autorización (la) (n.)	*Authorization*
Autorizar (v.)	*Authorize*
Axila (la) (n.)	*Armpit*
Ayudar (v.)	*Help*
Ayunar (v.)	*Fast*
Bacteria (la) (n.)	*Bacteria*
Balanceado, a (adj.)	*Balanced*
Bañar (v.)	*Bathe*
Banco de sangre (el) (n.)	*Blood bank*
Banda adhesiva (la) (n.)	*Band aid*
Baño (el) (n.)	*Bathroom*
Barba (la) (n.)	*Beard*
Barbilla (la) (n.)	*Chin*
Barros (los) (n.)	*Black heads*
Básico, a (adj.)	*Basic*
Bata (la) (n.)	*Robe*

Español	Inglés
Batería (la) (n.)	*Battery*
Bazo (el) (n.)	*Spleen*
Bebé (el) (n.)	*Baby*
Beber (v.)	*Drink*
Benadryl (n.)	*Benadryl*
Benigno, a (adj.)	*Benign*
Berrinche (el) (n.)	*Temper tantrum*
Bien (el) (n.) (adv.)	*Well*
Bienestar (el) (n.)	*Well being*
Bigote (el) (n.)	*Mustache*
Bilis (la) (n.)	*Bile*
Biopsia (la) (n.)	*Biopsy*
Bizco, a (adj.)	*Cross eyed*
Blando, a (adj.)	*Bland*
Blusa (la) (n.)	*Blouse*
Boca (la) (n.)	*Mouth*
Boca abajo (adv.)	*Face down*
Boca arriba (adv.)	*Face up*
Bochornos (los) (n.)	*Hot flashes*
Bocio (el) (n.)	*Goiter*
Bola (la) (n.)	*Lump*
Bolsa de agua (la) (n.)	*Water bag*
Borroso, a (adj.)	*Blurry*
Botiquín (el) (n.)	*Medicine chest*
Botón (el) (n.)	*Button*
Brazo (el) (n.)	*Arm*
Bronquitis (la) (n.)	*Bronchitis*
Bulimia (la) (n.)	*Bulimia*
Cabeza (la) (n.)	*Head*
Cadáver (el) (n.)	*Cadaver*
Cadera (la) (n.)	*Hip*
Caer (v.)	*Fall*
Café (el) (n.)	*Coffee*
Cafeína (la) (n.)	*Caffeine*

Cajero, a (n.)	*Cashier*
Cajetilla (la) (n.)	*Pack of cigarettes*
Calambre (el) (n.)	*Cramp*
Calcio (el) (n.)	*Calcium*
Caldo (el) (n.)	*Broth*
Callo (el) (n.)	*Callus*
Calma (la) (n.)	*Calm*
Calmante (el) (n.)	*Tranquilizer*
Caloría (la) (n.)	*Calorie*
Cama (la) (n.)	*Bed*
Camilla (la) (n.)	*Guerney*
Caminar (v.)	*Walk*
Campanilla (la) (n.)	*Uvula*
Canal en la naríz (el) (n.)	*Nasal canal*
Cáncer (el) (n.)	*Cancer*
Cansado, a (adj.)	*Tired*
Cansancio (el) (n.)	*Tiredness*
Cantidad (la) (n.)	*Amount*
Capilares (los) (n.)	*Capillaries*
Cápsula (la) (n.)	*Capsule*
Cara (la) (n.)	*Face*
Carbohidrato (el) (n.)	*Carbohydrate*
Carcinogénico, a (adj.)	*Carcinogenic*
Cardíaco, a (adj.)	*Cardiac*
Cardiología (la) (n.)	*Cardiology*
Cardiólogo, a (n.)	*Cardiologist*
Cardiopulmonar (adj.)	*Cardiopulmonary*
Cardiovascular (adj.)	*Cardiovascular*
Carie (la) (n.)	*Cavity*
Cartílago (el) (n.)	*Cartilage*
Casado, a (adj.)	*Married*
Caso (el) (n.)	*Case*
Caspa (la) (n.)	*Dandruff*
Cataratas (las) (n.)	*Cataracts*

Causa (la) (n.)	*Cause*
Cavidad nasal (la) (n.)	*Sinus*
Cejas (las) (n.)	*Eyebrows*
Célula (la) (n.)	*Cell*
Cerebelo (el) (n.)	*Cerebellum*
Cerebro (el) (n.)	*Brain*
Cerebrovascular (adj.)	*Cerebrovascular*
Cerilla (la) (n.)	*Earwax*
Cerviz (la) (n.)	*Cervix*
Cesárea (la) (n.)	*Cesarean*
Chancro (el) (n.)	*Canker*
Chaqueta (la) (n.)	*Jacket*
Chocar (v.)	*Collide*
Cicatriz (la) (n.)	*Scar*
Ciego, a (adj.)	*Blind*
Cigarros (los) (n.)	*Cigarettes*
Cintura (la) (n.)	*Waist*
Circulación (la) (n.)	*Circulation*
Circuncisión (la) (n.)	*Circumcision*
Cirugía (la) (n.)	*Surgery*
Cirujano (el) (n.)	*Surgeon*
Cistitis (la) (n.)	*Cystitis*
Cita (la) (n.)	*Appointment*
Claramente (adv.)	*Clearly*
Claro, a (adj.)	*Clear*
Clavícula (la) (n.)	*Collar Bone*
Clínica (la) (n.)	*Clinic*
Clítoris (el) (n.)	*Clitoris*
Cloro (el) (n.)	*Bleach*
Coagulación (la) (n.)	*Coagulation*
Cobija (la) (n.)	*Blanket*
Cocinado, a (adj.)	*Cooked*
Cocinar (v.)	*Cook*
Codo (el) (n.)	*Elbow*

Cognitivo, a (adj.)	*Cognitive*
Colesterol (el) (n.)	*Cholesterol*
Cólico (el) (n.)	*Cramp*
Colitis (la) (n.)	*Colitis*
Colon (el) (n.)	*Colon*
Color (el) (n.)	*Color*
Columna vertebral (la) (n.)	*Spine*
Coma (el) (n.)	*Coma*
Comer (v.)	*Eat*
Comezón (la) (n.)	*Itch*
Comida (la) (n.)	*Food*
Cómodo, a (adj.)	*Comfortable*
Compañero, a sexual (n.)	*Sexual partner*
Compañía de seguros (la) (n.)	*Insurance company*
Compulsión (la) (n.)	*Compulsion*
Compulsivo, a (adj.)	*Compulsive*
Concebir (v.)	*Conceive*
Condimentado, a (adj.)	*Spicy*
Condón (el) (n.)	*Condom*
Conducta (la) (n.)	*Behavior*
Confirmar (v.)	*Confirm*
Confusión (la) (n.)	*Confusion*
Congestión (la) (n.)	*Congestion*
Conjuntivitis (la) (n.)	*Conjunctivitis*
Conocer (v.)	*Know*
Consejo (el) (n.)	*Advice*
Consentir (v.)	*Consent*
Constantemente (adv.)	*Constantly*
Constipación (la) (n.)	*Constipation*
Consultar (v.)	*Consult*
Consultorio (el) (n.)	*Doctor's office*
Contagio (el) (n.)	*Contagious*
Contagioso, a (adj.)	*Contagious*
Contar (v.)	*Count*

Contener (v.)	*Contain*
Continuar (v.)	*Continue*
Contra (prep.)	*Against*
Contracción (la) (n.)	*Contraction*
Control (el) (n.)	*Control*
Control de la natalidad (el) (n.)	*Birth control*
Contusión (la) (n.)	*Contusion*
Convulsiones (las) (n.)	*Convulsions*
Coordinador, a (n.) (adj.)	*Coordinator*
Coraje (el) (n.)	*Anger*
Corazón (el) (n.)	*Heart*
Cordón umbilical (el) (n.)	*Umbilical cord*
Córnea (la) (n.)	*Cornea*
Corona (la) (n.)	*Crown*
Correcto, a (adj.)	*Correct*
Cortada (la) (n.)	*Cut*
Corticosteroides (los) (n.)	*Corticosteroids*
Cortina (la) (n.)	*Curtain*
Corva (la) (n.)	*Back of the knee*
Cosmético (el) (n.) (adj.)	*Cosmetic*
Costilla (la) (n.)	*Rib*
Costra (la) (n.)	*Scab*
Coxis (el) (n.)	*Coccyx*
Coyuntura (la) (n.)	*Joint*
Cráneo (el) (n.)	*Skull*
Credencial (la) (n.)	*Credential*
Creer (v.)	*Believe*
Crema (la) (n.)	*Cream*
Cromosoma (el) (n.)	*Chromosome*
Crónico, a (adj.)	*Chronic*
Crup (el) (n.)	*Croup*
Cruz (la) (n.)	*Cross*
Cuadra (la) (n.)	*Block*
Cuadriplegia (la) (n.)	*Quadriplegic*

Cubrir (v.)	*Cover*
Cucharada (la) (n.)	*Spoonful*
Cuello (el) (n.)	*Neck*
Cuenta (la) (n.)	*Bill*
Cuero cabelludo (el) (n.)	*Scalp*
Cuidado (el) (n.)	*Care*
Cuidados Intensivos (los) (n.)	*Intensive care*
Cuna (la) (n.)	*Crib*
Cura (la) (n.)	*Cure*
Curita (el) (n.)	*Adhesive bandage*
Cutis (el) (n.)	*Complexion*
Daltonismo (el) (n.)	*Color blind*
Daño (el) (n.)	*Damage*
Dar de alta (v.)	*Discharge*
Dar pecho (v.)	*Breast feed*
Debajo (adv.)	*Under*
Débil (adj.)	*Weak*
Debilidad (la) (n.)	*Weakness*
Decidir (v.)	*Decide*
Dedo (el) (n.)	*Finger*
Dedo del pie (el) (n.)	*Toe*
Deformidad (la) (n.)	*Deformity*
Delgado, a (adj.)	*Thin*
Delirio (el) (n.)	*Delirium*
Demencia (la) (n.)	*Dementia*
Dentadura (la) (n.)	*Dentures*
Dental (adj.)	*Dental*
Dentista (el-la) (n.)	*Dentist*
Departamento (el) (n.)	*Department*
Depresión (la) (n.)	*Depression*
Derecho (el) (n.)	*Right*
Dermatitis (la) (n.)	*Dermatitis*
Dermatólogo (el-la) (n.)	*Dermatologist*
Desastre (el) (n.)	*Disaster*

Español	Inglés
Descanso (el) (n.)	*Rest*
Descongestionante (n.) (adj.)	*Decongestant*
Desde (prep.)	*From*
Deshidratación (la) (n.)	*Dehydration*
Desinfectar (v.)	*Disinfect*
Desintoxicación (la) (n.)	*Detox*
Desmayo (el) (n.)	*Faint*
Desprendimiento (el) (n.)	*Detachment*
Destruir (v.)	*Destroy*
Desvestir (v.)	*Undress*
Detergente (el) (n.)	*Detergent*
Determinar (v.)	*Determine*
Diabetes (la) (n.)	*Diabetes*
Diabético, a (n.) (adj.)	*Diabetic*
Diafragma (el) (n.)	*Diaphragm*
Diagnosis (la) (n.)	*Diagnosis*
Diagnóstico (el) (n.)	*Diagnostic*
Diálisis (la) (n.)	*Dialysis*
Diario, a (adj.)	*Daily*
Diarrea (la) (n.)	*Diarrhea*
Diente (el) (n.)	*Tooth*
Diente de Leche (el) (n.)	*Baby tooth*
Diestro, a (adj.)	*Right handed*
Dieta (la) (n.)	*Diet*
Dietista (n.)	*Dietitian*
Diferente (adj.)	*Different*
Difícil (adj.)	*Difficult*
Dificultad (la) (n.)	*Difficulty*
Difteria (la) (n.)	*Diphtheria*
Digerir (v.)	*Digest*
Digestivo (el) (n.)	*Digestive*
Dilatado, a (adj.)	*Dilated*
Dirección (la) (n.)	*Address*
Disciplina (la) (n.)	*Discipline*

Disco (el) (n.)	*Disk*
Dislocación (la) (n.)	*Dislocation*
Disminuir (v.)	*Diminish*
Dispositivo intrauterino (el) (n.)	*IUD*
Doblar (v.)	*Bend*
Doctor, ra (n.)	*Doctor*
Dolor (el) (n.)	*Ache*
Dolor de cabeza (el) (n.)	*Head ache*
Dolor de garganta (el) (n.)	*Sore throat*
Dolores de parto (los) (n.)	*Labor pains*
Doloroso, a (adj.)	*Painful*
Doméstico, a (adj.)	*Domestic*
Dominante (adj.)	*Dominant*
Dormido (adj.)	*Asleep*
Dormir (v.)	*Sleep*
Dorsal (adj.)	*Dorsal*
Dosis (la) (n.)	*Dosage*
Droga (la) (n.)	*Drug*
Drogadicto, a (n.) (adj.)	*Drug addict*
Duelo (el) (n.)	*Grief*
Dulce (adj.)	*Candy*
Duodeno (el) (n.)	*Duodenum*
Duro (adj.)	*Hard*
Eczema (el) (n.)	*Eczema*
Edad (la) (n.)	*Age*
Edema (el) (n.)	*Edema*
Edificio (el) (n.)	*Building*
Efectivo, a (adj.)	*Effective*
Efecto colateral (el) (n.)	*Side effect*
Ejercicio (el) (n.)	*Exercise*
Eléctrico, a (adj.)	*Electric*
Electrocardiograma (el) (n.)	*Electrocardiogram, EKG*
Elevador (el) (n.)	*Elevator*
Embarazada (la) (adj.)	*Pregnant*

Embarazo (el) (n.)	*Pregnancy*
Embolia (la) (n.)	*Stroke*
Emergencia (la) (n.)	*Emergency*
Empezar (v.)	*Begin*
Empujar (v.)	*Push*
Encefalitis (la) (n.)	*Encephalitis*
Encía (la) (n.)	*Gum*
Encopresis (la) (n.)	*Encopresis*
Endocrinólogo (el-la) (n.)	*Endocrinologist*
Endoscopía (la) (n.)	*Endoscopy*
Endoscopio (el) (n.)	*Endoscope*
Endurecimiento (el) (n.)	*Hardening*
Enema (la) (n.)	*Enema*
Enfermedad (la) (n.)	*Sickness*
Enfermedad mental (la) (n.)	*Mental illness*
Enfermera (la) (n.)	*Nurse*
Enfermería (la) (n.)	*Nursing department*
Enfermo, a (n.)	*Sick*
Enfisema (el) (n.)	*Emphysema*
Entrada (la) (n.)	*Entrance*
Entrenamiento (el) (n.)	*Training*
Entrepierna (la) (n.)	*Groin*
Entumecido, a (adj.)	*Numb*
Enuresis (la) (n.)	*Enuresis*
Envenenamiento (el) (n.)	*Poisoning*
Enzima (la) (n.)	*Enzyme*
Epidermis (la) (n.)	*Epidermis*
Epigastrio (el) (n.)	*Pit of Stomach*
Epilepsia (la) (n.)	*Epilepsy*
Epinefrina (la) (n.)	*Epinephrine*
Equipo (el) (n.)	*Equipment*
Erección (la) (n.)	*Erection*
Eructar (v.)	*Burp*
Escalofrío (el) (n.)	*Chill*

Escápula (la) (n.)	*Shoulder blade*
Escroto (el) (n.)	*Scrotum*
Escupir (v.)	*Spit*
Escusado	*Toilet*
Esfuerzo (el) (n.)	*Effort*
Esófago (el) (n.)	*Esophagus*
Espalda (la) (n.)	*Back*
Espasmo (el) (n.)	*Spasm*
Especialidad (la) (n.)	*Specialty*
Esperar (v.)	*Wait*
Espermicida (el) (n.) (adj.)	*Spermicide*
Espina dorsal (la) (n.)	*Dorsal spine*
Espinilla (la) (n.)	*Black head*
Espinilla (la) (n.)	*Shin of leg*
Espiritualidad (la) (n.)	*Spirituality*
Esponja (la) (n.)	*Sponge*
Esposa (la) (n.)	*Wife*
Esposo (el) (n.)	*Husband*
Espuma (la) (n.)	*Foam*
Esqueleto (el) (n.)	*Skeleton*
Esterilidad (la) (n.)	*Sterility*
Esterilización (la) (n.)	*Sterilization*
Esternón (el) (n.)	*Breast bone*
Esteroides (los) (adj.)	*Steroids*
Estetoscopio (el) (n.)	*Stethoscope*
Estómago (el) (n.)	*Stomach*
Estrecho, a (adj.)	*Narrow*
Estrógeno (el) (n.)	*Estrogen*
Estudio (el) (n.)	*Study*
Estupor (el) (n.)	*Stupor*
Evacuación intestinal (la) (n.)	*Bowel movement*
Examen (el) (n.)	*Check-up*
Examen vaginal (el) (n.)	*Pap smear test*
Exceso de peso (el) (n.)	*Overweight*

Excremento (el) (n.)	*Stool*
Exhausto, a (adj.)	*Exhaust*
Expectorante (adj.)	*Expectorant*
Expediente médico (el) (n.)	*Medical chart*
Extraer (v.)	*Extract*
Extremidades (las) (n.)	*Limbs*
Eyaculación (la) (n.)	*Ejaculation*
Factores (los) (n.)	*Factors*
Familia (la) (n.)	*Family*
Farmacia (la) (n.)	*Pharmacy*
Fatiga (la) (n.)	*Fatigue*
Fecha (la) (n.)	*Date*
Fémur (el) (n.)	*Femur*
Fértil (adj.)	*Fertile*
Feto (el) (n.)	*Fetus*
Fibra (la) (n.)	*Fiber*
Fiebre (la) (n.)	*Fever*
Fiebre de heno (la) (n.)	*Hay fever*
Fiebre escarlatina (la) (n.)	*Scarlet fever*
Fiebre reumática (la) (n.)	*Rheumatic fever*
Fielmente (adv.)	*Faithfully*
Finalmente (adv.)	*Finally*
Firma (la) (n.)	*Signature*
Físico, a (adj.)	*Physical*
Fisioterapia (la) (n.)	*Physiotherapy*
Flema (la) (n.)	*Sputum*
Fluoroscopía (la) (n.)	*Fluoroscopy*
Fobia (la) (n.)	*Phobia*
Folleto (el) (n.)	*Pamphlet*
Fontanela (la) (n.)	*Fontanelle*
Fórceps (el) (n.)	*Forceps*
Forma (la) (n.)	*Form*
Fórmula (la) (n.)	*Formula*
Fosas nasales (las) (n.)	*Nostril*

Fractura (la) (n.)	*Fracture*
Frasco (el) (n.)	*Bottle*
Frecuente (adv.)	*Frequently*
Frente (la) (n.)	*Forehead*
Fricción (la) (n.)	*Friction*
Frigidez (la) (n.)	*Frigidity*
Fumar (v.)	*Smoke*
Gafas (las) (n.)	*Eye glasses*
Gamaglobulina (la) (n.)	*Gamma globulin*
Ganglio (el) (n.)	*Ganglion*
Ganglio linfático (el) (n.)	*Lymph node*
Gangrena (la) (n.)	*Gangrene*
Garganta (la) (n.)	*Throat*
Gárgaras (las) (n.)	*Gargle*
Gas (el) (n.)	*Gas*
Gasa (la) (n.)	*Gauze*
Gástrico, a (adj.)	*Gastric*
Gastritis (la) (n.)	*Gastritis*
Gastroenteritis (la) (n.)	*Gastroenteritis*
Gastrointestinal (adj.)	*Gastrointestinal*
Gatear (v.)	*To crawl*
Gene (el) (n.)	*Gene*
General (el) (n.)	*General*
Genético, a (adj.)	*Genetic*
Genital (adj.)	*Genital*
Genitales (los) (n.)	*Genitals*
Geriatra (el-la) (n.)	*Geriatric*
Germen (el) (n.)	*Germ*
Gestación (la) (n.)	*Gestation*
Ginecólogo (el-la) (n.)	*Gynecologist*
Gingivitis (la) (n.)	*Gingivitis*
Glándula (la) (n.)	*Gland*
Glándula lagrimal (la) (n.)	*Lachrymal gland*
Glándula pituitaria (la) (n.)	*Pituitary gland*

Español	Inglés
Glaucoma (el) (n.)	*Glaucoma*
Globo (el) (n.)	*Balloon*
Globulina (la) (n.)	*Globulin*
Glucosa (la) (n.)	*Glucose*
Golpear (v.)	*Hit*
Gonorrea (la) (n.)	*Gonorrhea*
Gota (la) (n.)	*Gout*
Gotas (las) (n.)	*Drops*
Gotas para la nariz (las) (n.)	*Nose drops*
Gotero (el) (n.)	*Dropper*
Grado (el) (n.)	*Degree*
Grande (adj.)	*Large*
Grano (el) (n.)	*Pimple*
Grasa (la) (n.)	*Fat*
Grasoso, a (adj.)	*Oily*
Grave (adj.)	*Serious*
Gripa (la) (n.)	*Cold*
Grumo (el) (n.)	*Curd*
Grupo (el) (n.)	*Group*
Hábitos (los) (n.)	*Habits*
Hacia abajo (adv.)	*Downward*
Hacia adelante (adv.)	*Forward*
Hacia atrás (adv.)	*Backwards*
Halitosis (la) (n.)	*Halitosis*
Heces (las) (n.)	*Feces*
Helado (el) (n.)	*Iced*
Hematoma (el) (n.)	*Hematoma*
Hemiplejía (la) (n.)	*Hemiplegia*
Hemoglobina (la) (n.)	*Hemoglobin*
Hemorragia (la) (n.)	*Hemorrhage*
Hemorroides (las) (n.)	*Hemorrhoids*
Hepático, a (adj.)	*Hepatic*
Hepatitis (la) (n.)	*Hepatitis*
Hereditario, a (adj.)	*Hereditary*

Herida (la) (n.)	*Injury*
Herido, a (n.) (adj.)	*Injured Person*
Hermana (la) (n.)	*Sister*
Hermano (el) (n.)	*Brother*
Hernia (la) (n.)	*Hernia*
Herpes (el) (n.)	*Herpes*
Hielo (el) (n.)	*Ice*
Hígado (el) (n.)	*Liver*
Hija (la) (n.)	*Daughter*
Hijo (el) (n.)	*Son*
Hilo dental (el) (n.)	*Dental-floss*
Hiperactivo, a (adj.)	*Hyperactive*
Hiperglucemia (la) (n.)	*Hyperglycemia*
Hipertensión (la) (n.)	*Hypertension*
Hiperventilación (la) (n.)	*Hyperventilation*
Hipo (el) (n.)	*Hiccups*
Hipocondría (la) (n.)	*Hypochondria*
Hipotálamo (el) (n.)	*Hypothalamus*
Hipotermia (la) (n.)	*Hypothermia*
Hirviendo (adv.)	*Boiling*
Histerectomía (la) (n.)	*Hysterectomy*
Historia clínica (la) (n.)	*Medical-history*
Hombre (el) (n.)	*Man*
Hombro (el) (n.)	*Shoulder*
Hondo, a (adj.)	*Deep*
Hongo (el) (n.)	*Yeast*
Hormona (la) (n.)	*Hormone*
Hospital (el) (n.)	*Hospital*
Hueso (el) (n.)	*Bone*
Huevo (el) (n.)	*Egg*
Ibuprofen (el) (n.)	*Ibuprofen*
Ideopático, a (adj.)	*Idiopathic*
Impétigo (el) (n.)	*Impetigo*
Importante (adv.)	*Important*

Español	Inglés
Impotencia (la) (n.)	*Impotence*
Incapacidad (la) (n.)	*Disability*
Incisión (la) (n.)	*Incision*
Incontinencia (la) (n.)	*Incontinence*
Incubación (la) (n.)	*Incubation*
Incubador (el) (n.)	*Incubator*
Indicación (la) (n.)	*Indication*
Indicar (v.)	*Indicate*
Índice (el) (n.)	*Index finger*
Indigestión (la) (n.)	*Indigestion*
Infarto (el) (n.)	*Heart attack*
Infección (la) (n.)	*Infection*
Infeccioso, a (adj.)	*Infectious*
Infectar (v.)	*Infect*
Infértil (adj.)	*Infertile*
Inflamado, a (adj.)	*Swollen*
Informe (el) (n.)	*Report*
Inhalador (el) (n.)	*Inhaler*
Inmediatamente (adv.)	*Immediately*
Inmovilizar (v.)	*Immobilize*
Inmune (adj.)	*Immune*
Inmunización (la) (n.)	*Immunization*
Inmunológico, a (adj.)	*Immunology*
Inmunoterapia (la) (n.)	*Immunotherapy*
Insecticida (el) (n.)	*Insecticide*
Insectos (los) (n.)	*Insects*
Inseminación (la) (n.)	*Insemination*
Insertar (v.)	*Insert*
Insolación (la) (n.)	*Sunstroke*
Insomnio (el) (n.)	*Insomnia*
Insoportable (adj.)	*Unbearable*
Instrucción (la) (n.)	*Instruction*
Insulina (la) (n.)	*Insulin*
Intensivo, a (adj.)	*Intensive*

Vocabulario

Interacción (la) (n.)	*Interaction*
Internar (v.)	*Admit*
Intervención (la) (n.)	*Surgical intervention*
Intestinos (los) (n.)	*Intestines*
Intolerancia (la) (n.)	*Intolerance*
Intoxicación (la) (n.)	*Intoxication*
Intravenoso, a (adj.)	*Intravenous*
Inyección (la) (n.)	*Injection*
Inyectar (v.)	*Inject*
Iris (el) (n.)	*Iris*
Irregular (adj.)	*Irregular*
Irritación (la) (n.)	*Irritation*
Izquierdo, a (adj.)	*Left*
Jabón (el) (n.)	*Soap*
Jalea (la) (n.)	*Jelly*
Jarabe (el) (n.)	*Syrup*
Juanete (el) (n.)	*Bunion*
Jugo (el) (n.)	*Juice*
Kaopectate (el) (n.)	*Kaopectate*
Labio (el) (n.)	*Lip*
Labios (los) (n.)	*Lips*
Laboratorio (el) (n.)	*Laboratory*
Laceración (la) (n.)	*Laceration*
Lácteo, a (adj.)	*Dairy*
Lado (el) (n.)	*Side*
Laringe (la) (n.)	*Larynx*
Laringitis (la) (n.)	*Laryngitis*
Lastimar (v.)	*Hurt*
Latido (el) (n.)	*Heart beat*
Lavar (v.)	*Wash*
Laxante (adj.)	*Laxative*
Leche (la) (n.)	*Milk*
Leche descremada (la) (n.)	*Non fat milk*
Lejos (adv.)	*Far*

Español	Inglés
Lengua (la) (n.)	*Tongue*
Lentamente (adv.)	*Slowly*
Lentes de contacto (los) (n.)	*Contact lenses*
Lento, a (adj.)	*Slow*
Lesión (la) (n.)	*Lesion*
Letargo (el) (n.)	*Lethargic*
Leucemia (la) (n.)	*Leukemia*
Levantar (v.)	*Raise*
Levantarse (v. r.)	*To get up*
Líbido (la) (n.)	*Libido*
Libra (la) (n.)	*Pound*
Ligadura (la) (n.)	*Tourniquet*
Ligamento (el) (n.)	*Ligament*
Ligero, a (adj.)	*Light*
Limitación (la) (n.)	*Limitation*
Limpio, a (adj.)	*Clean*
Linfático, a (adj.)	*Lymphatic*
Liposucción (la) (n.)	*Liposuction*
Líquido (el) (n.)	*Liquid*
Lista (la) (n.)	*List*
Llaga (la) (n.)	*Sore*
Llamar (v.)	*Call*
Llegar (v.)	*Arrive*
Llenar (v.)	*Fill out*
Local (adj.)	*Local*
Localizado, a (adj.)	*Localized*
Loción (la) (n.)	*Lotion*
Locura (la) (n.)	*Insanity*
Lubricar (v.)	*Lubricate*
Lumbar (adj.)	*Lower back*
Lunar (el) (n.)	*Mole*
Magnesia (la) (n.)	*Magnesia*
Malestar (el) (n.)	*Discomfort*
Maligno, a (adj.)	*Malignant*

Malo, a (adj.)	*Bad*
Malparto (el) (n.)	*Miscarriage*
Mamá (la) (n.)	*Mother*
Mamadera (la) (n.)	*Baby bottle*
Mamograma (el) (n.)	*Mammogram*
Mandíbula (la) (n.)	*Jaw*
Manera (la) (n.)	*Manner*
Manía (la) (n.)	*Mania*
Mano (la) (n.)	*Hand*
Mantequilla (la) (n.)	*Butter*
Manzana (la) (n.)	*Apple*
Manzanilla (la) (n.)	*Camomile*
Maquillaje (el) (n.)	*Make up*
Marcapaso (el) (n.)	*Pacemaker*
Mareo (el) (n.)	*Dizziness*
Masaje (el) (n.)	*Massage*
Masticar (v.)	*Chew*
Matriz (la) (n.)	*Womb*
Medianoche (la) (n.)	*Midnight*
Medicamentos (los) (n.)	*Medications*
Medicina (la) (n.)	*Medicine*
Médico (el) (n.)	*Doctor, MD*
Medio (el) (n.)	*Middle*
Medir (v.)	*Measure*
Médula (la) (n.)	*Medulla*
Médula ósea (la) (n.)	*Bone marrow*
Mejor (adj.)	*Better*
Mejorar (v.)	*Improve*
Melanoma (el) (n.)	*Melanoma*
Mellizos (los) (n.) (adj.)	*Twins*
Membrana (la) (n.)	*Membrane*
Meningitis (la) (n.)	*Meningitis*
Menopausia (la) (n.)	*Menopause*
Menor (adj.)	*Minor*

Menstruación (la) (n.)	*Menstruation*
Mental (adj.)	*Mental*
Mercurocromo (el) (n.)	*Mercurochrome*
Mes (el) (n.)	*Month*
Metabolismo (el) (n.)	*Metabolism*
Método (el) (n.)	*Method*
Microbios (los) (n.)	*Microbes*
Miedo (el) (n.)	*Fear*
Miel (la) (n.)	*Honey*
Migraña (la) (n.)	*Migraine*
Mineral (el) (n.)	*Mineral*
Miope (n.) (adj.)	*Near sighted*
Mirar (v.)	*Look*
Mitad (la) (n.)	*Half*
Moco (el) (n.)	*Mucous*
Moderado, a (adj.)	*Moderate*
Molestia (la) (n.)	*Trouble*
Mononucleosis (la) (n.)	*Mononucleosis*
Morder (v.)	*Bite*
Moretón (el) (n.)	*Bruise*
Mosquito (el) (n.)	*Mosquito*
Muchacha (la) (n.)	*Young girl*
Muchacho (el) (n.)	*Young man*
Mucosa (la) (n.)	*Mucous membrane*
Muela (la) (n.)	*Molar*
Muela del juicio (la) (n.)	*Wisdom tooth*
Muerte (la) (n.)	*Death*
Muestra (la) (n.)	*Sample*
Mujer (la) (n.)	*Woman*
Muletas (las) (n.)	*Crutches*
Muñeca (la) (n.)	*Wrist*
Músculo (el) (n.)	*Muscle*
Musculoesquelético (el) (n.)	*Skeletal muscles*
Muslo (el) (n.)	*Thigh*

Nacimiento (el) (n.)	*Birth*
Nalgas (las) (n.)	*Buttocks*
Nariz (la) (n.)	*Nose*
Nasal (adj.)	*Nasal*
Natal (adj.)	*Native*
Natural (adj.)	*Natural*
Náusea (la) (n.)	*Nausea*
Necesario, a (adj.)	*Necessary*
Necesitar (v.)	*Need*
Negativo, a (adj.)	*Negative*
Neonato (el) (n.)	*Neonate*
Nervio (el) (n.)	*Nerve*
Nervioso, a (adj.)	*Nervous*
Neuralgia (la) (n.)	*Neuralgia*
Neurólogo (el-la) (n.)	*Neurologist*
Neurona (la) (n.)	*Neuron*
Neurotransmisores (los) (n.)	*Neurotransmitters*
Nicotina (la) (n.)	*Nicotine*
Niño, a (n.) (adj.)	*Child*
Noche (la) (n.)	*Night*
Nombre (el) (n.)	*Name*
Normal (adj.)	*Normal*
Normalmente (adv.)	*Normally*
Notar (v.)	*Notice*
Novocaína (la) (n.)	*Novocain*
Nuca (la) (n.)	*Back of the head*
Núcleo (el) (n.)	*Nuclear*
Nudillo (el) (n.)	*Knuckle*
Nudos linfáticos (los) (n.)	*Lymphatic nodes*
Nuez de Adán (la) (n.)	*Adam's apple*
Nutrición (la) (n.)	*Nutrition*
Obesidad (la) (n.)	*Obesity*
Objeto (el) (n.)	*Object*
Obstruido, a (adj.)	*Obstructed*

Español	Inglés
Occipital (adj.)	*Occipital*
Ocular (adj.)	*Ocular*
Oculista (el-la) (n.)	*Oculist*
Ocupación (la) (n.)	*Occupation*
Ocupado, a (adj.)	*Busy*
Oficina (la) (n.)	*Office*
Oftalmólogo (el-la) (n.)	*Ophthalmologist*
Oído (el) (n.)	*Ear*
Ojo (el) (n.)	*Eye*
Olfatorio, a (adj.)	*Olfactory*
Olor (el) (n.)	*Odor*
Ombligo (el) (n.)	*Belly button*
Oncólogo (el-la) (n.)	*Oncologist*
Operación (la) (n.)	*Operation*
Operar (v.)	*Operate*
Opresión (la) (n.)	*Tightness*
Óptico, a (adj.)	*Optical*
Optimismo (el) (n.)	*Optimism*
Optométrico, a (adj.)	*Optometrist*
Oral (adj.)	*Oral*
Órbita (la) (n.)	*Orbit*
Órgano (el) (n.)	*Organ*
Orgasmo (el) (n.)	*Orgasm*
Orina (la) (n.)	*Urine*
Orinar (v.)	*Urinate*
Ortodoncia (la) (n.)	*Orthodontics*
Ortodoncista (el-la) (n.)	*Orthodontist*
Ortopedia (la) (n.)	*Orthopedics*
Ortopedista (el-la) (n.)	*Orthopedist*
Orzuelo (el) (n.)	*Sty*
Oscuridad (la) (n.)	*Darkness*
Oscuro, a (adj.)	*Dark*
Osteoporosis (la) (n.)	*Osteoporosis*
Ovario (el) (n.)	*Ovary*

Ovulación (la) (n.)	*Ovulation*
Oxígeno (el) (n.)	*Oxygen*
Paciente (el) (n.)	*Patient*
Paciente externo (el, la) (n.)	*Outpatient*
Padre (el) (n.)	*Father*
Padres (los) (n.)	*Parents*
Pagar (v.)	*Pay*
Pago (el) (n.)	*Payment*
Paladar (el) (n.)	*Palate*
Pálido, a (adj.)	*Pale*
Palpitaciones (las) (n.)	*Palpitations*
Pañales (los) (n.)	*Diapers*
Páncreas (el) (n.)	*Pancreas*
Pánico (el) (n.)	*Panic*
Pantorrilla (la) (n.)	*Calf*
Papel (el) (n.)	*Paper*
Paperas (las) (n.)	*Mumps*
Parálisis (la) (n.)	*Paralysis*
Paramédico (el) (n.)	*Paramedic*
Paranoia (la) (n.)	*Paranoia*
Paraplejía (la) (n.)	*Paraplegia*
Parásito (el) (n.)	*Parasite*
Parcial (adj.)	*Partial*
Pareja (la) (n.)	*Couple*
Pariente (el) (n.)	*Relative*
Paro cardíaco (el) (n.)	*Cardiac arrest*
Párpado (el) (n.)	*Eyelid*
Partera (la) (n.)	*Midwife*
Parir (v.)	*Give birth*
Parto (el) (n.)	*Delivery*
Parto (el) (n.)	*Labor*
Pasillo (el) (n.)	*Hallway*
Pasta dentífrica (la) (n.)	*Toothpaste*
Pastel (el) (n.)	*Cake*

Pastilla (la) (n.)	*Pill*
Patógeno, a (adj.)	*Pathogenic*
Patología (la) (n.)	*Pathology*
Patológico, a (adj.)	*Pathological*
Pecho (el) (n.)	*Chest*
Pedialyte (el) (n.)	*Pedialyte*
Pediatra (el-la) (n.)	*Pediatrician*
Peligroso, a (adj.)	*Dangerous*
Pelo (el) (n.)	*Hair*
Pelvis (la) (n.)	*Pelvis*
Pene (el) (n.)	*Penis*
Penicilina (la) (n.)	*Penicillin*
Pensamiento (el) (n.)	*Thought*
Peor (el) (n.)	*Worst*
Pérdida (la) (n.)	*Loss*
Perfume (el) (n.)	*Perfume*
Pericardio (el) (n.)	*Pericardium*
Período (el) (n.)	*Period*
Peritonitis (la) (n.)	*Peritonitis*
Peróxido (el) (n.)	*Peroxide*
Persistente (adj.)	*Persistent*
Persona (la) (n.)	*Person*
Pesadilla (la) (n.)	*Nightmare*
Pesado, a (adj.)	*Heavy*
Pesar (v.)	*Weigh*
Pescado (el) (n.)	*Fish*
Pesimismo (el) (n.)	*Pessimism*
Peso (el) (n.)	*Weight*
Pestaña (la) (n.)	*Eyelash*
Pezón (el) (n.)	*Nipple*
Pie (el) (n.)	*Foot*
Pie de atleta (el) (n.)	*Athletes foot*
Piel (la) (n.)	*Skin*
Pierna (la) (n.)	*Leg*

Pigmento (el) (n.)	*Pigment*
Pinchar (v.)	*Prick*
Pinza de cejas (la) (n.)	*Tweezers*
Piojos (los) (n.)	*Lice*
Piquete (el) (n.)	*Pinch*
Placebo (el) (n.)	*Placebo*
Placenta (la) (n.)	*Placenta*
Plaga (la) (n.)	*Plague*
Planificación (la) (n.)	*Planning*
Planta del pie (la) (n.)	*Sole*
Plasma (el) (n.)	*Plasma*
Polen (el) (n.)	*Pollen*
Poliomielitis (la) (n.)	*Polio*
Póliza (la) (n.)	*Policy*
Porción (la) (n.)	*Portion*
Poros (los) (n.)	*Pores*
Positivo, a (adj.)	*Positive*
Postparto (el) (n.)	*Postpartum*
Postura (la) (n.)	*Posture*
Potasio (el) (n.)	*Potassium*
Precaución (la) (n.)	*Precaution*
Preguntar (v.)	*Ask*
Prematuro, a (adj.)	*Premature*
Preocupación (la) (n.)	*Worry*
Preparación (la) (n.)	*Preparation*
Prescripción (la) (n.)	*Prescription*
Preservativos (los) (n.)	*Preservatives*
Presión (la) (n.)	*Pressure*
Presión sanguínea (la) (n.)	*Blood pressure*
Prevención (la) (n.)	*Prevention*
Primario, a (adj.)	*Primary*
Primeros auxilios (los) (n.)	*First aid*
Problema (el) (n.)	*Problem*
Profiláctico, a (adj.)	*Prophylactic*

Progesterona (la) (n.)	*Progesterone*
Pronóstico (el) (n.)	*Prognosis*
Próstata (la) (n.)	*Prostate gland*
Protección (la) (n.)	*Protection*
Proteína (la) (n.)	*Protein*
Prueba (la) (n.)	*Test*
Prueba de sangre (la) (n.)	*Blood test*
Psicología (la) (n.)	*Psychology*
Psicólogo (el-la) (n.)	*Psychologist*
Psicométrico, a (adj.)	*Psychometric*
Psicomotor, ra (adj.)	*Psychomotor*
Psicosis (la) (n.)	*Psychosis*
Psicosomático, a (adj.)	*Psychosomatic*
Psicoterapia (la) (n.)	*Psychotherapy*
Psiquiatra (el-la) (n.)	*Psychiatrist*
Psiquiatría (la) (n.)	*Psychiatry*
Pubertad (la) (n.)	*Puberty*
Pubis (el) (n.)	*Pubic area*
Puente (el) (n.)	*Bridge*
Pulgada (la) (n.)	*Inch*
Pulgar (el) (n.)	*Thumb*
Pulmón (el) (n.)	*Lung*
Pulmonía (la) (n.)	*Pneumonia*
Pulso (el) (n.)	*Pulse*
Punto (el) (n.)	*Stitch*
Punzada (la) (n.)	*Sharp pain*
Pupila (la) (n.)	*Pupil*
Pus (el) (n.)	*Pus*
Quejarse (v. r.)	*Complain*
Quemadura (la) (n.)	*Burn*
Quijada (la) (n.)	*Jaw*
Químico, a (adj.)	*Chemical*
Quimioterapia (la) (n.)	*Chemotherapy*
Quiste (el) (n.)	*Cyst*

Rabia (la) (n.)	*Rabies*
Radiación (la) (n.)	*Radiation*
Radiografía (la) (n.)	*X-ray*
Radiólogo (el-la) (n.)	*Radiologist*
Raíz (la) (n.)	*Root*
Raquianestesia (la) (n.)	*Spinal anesthesia*
Rasguño (el) (n.)	*Scratch*
Raspadura (la) (n.)	*Scrape*
Rasurar (v.)	*Shave*
Rayos equis (los) (n.)	*X-rays*
Reacción (la) (n.)	*Reaction*
Recaída (la) (n.)	*Relapse*
Recepcionista (el-la) (n.)	*Receptionist*
Recesivo, a (adj.)	*Recessive*
Recetar (v.)	*Prescribe*
Recién nacido, a (n.) (adj.)	*Newborn*
Recomendar (v.)	*Recommend*
Recto (el) (n.)	*Rectum*
Recurrente (adj.)	*Recurrent*
Reflejo (el) (n.)	*Reflex*
Regresar (v.)	*Return*
Regular (adj.)	*Regular*
Regularmente (adv.)	*Regularly*
Rehidratación (la) (n.)	*Rehydration*
Relación sexual (la) (n.)	*Sexual intercourse*
Relajación (la) (n.)	*Relaxation*
Relajarse (v. r.)	*Relax*
Remedio (el) (n.)	*Remedy*
Remedio casero (el) (n.)	*Home remedy*
Remisión (la) (n.)	*Remission*
Renal (adj.)	*Renal*
Repelentes (los) (n.)	*Repellent*
Repentino, a (adj.)	*Sudden*
Reporte médico (el) (n.)	*Medical report*

Rescate (el) (n.)	*Rescue*
Respirar (v.)	*Breathe*
Respiratorio (el) (n.)	*Respiratory*
Resultado (el) (n.)	*Result*
Resumen (el) (n.)	*Summary*
Retina (la) (n.)	*Retina*
Reumatismo (el) (n.)	*Rheumatism*
Reumatólogo (el-la) (n.)	*Rheumatologist*
Revisar (v.)	*Check*
Riesgo (el) (n.)	*Risk*
Riñón (el) (n.)	*Kidney*
Ritmo (el) (n.)	*Rhythm*
Ritmo cardíaco (el) (n.)	*Heart rhythm*
Rodilla (la) (n.)	*Knee*
Romper (v.)	*Break*
Ronco, a (adj.)	*Hoarse*
Ronquera (la) (n.)	*Hoarseness*
Ropa (la) (n.)	*Clothes*
Ropa interior (la) (n.)	*Underwear*
Rubeola (la) (n.)	*Rubella*
Ruido (el) (n.)	*Noise*
Ruptura (la) (n.)	*Rupture*
Sal (la) (n.)	*Salt*
Sala (la) (n.)	*Ward*
Sala de espera (la) (n.)	*Waiting room*
Sala de maternidad (la) (n.)	*Maternity ward*
Sala de parto (la) (n.)	*Delivery room*
Salir bien (v.)	*Come out fine*
Saliva (la) (n.)	*Saliva*
Salpullido (el) (n.)	*Rash*
Salud (la) (n.)	*Health*
Salud mental (la) (n.)	*Mental health*
Salvar (v.)	*Save*
Sangrar (v.)	*Bleed*

Sangre (la) (n.)	*Blood*
Sano, a (adj.)	*Healthy*
Sarampión (el) (n.)	*Measles*
Sarna (la) (n.)	*Scabies*
Sarro (el) (n.)	*Plaque*
Seco, a (adj.)	*Dry*
Secreción (la) (n.)	*Discharge*
Secretario (el) (n.)	*Secretary*
Secundario, a (adj.)	*Secondary*
Segunda opinión (la) (n.)	*Second opinion*
Seguro (el) (n.)	*Insurance*
Seguro social (el) (n.)	*Social security*
Semen (el) (n.)	*Semen*
Seno (el) (n.)	*Breast*
Sentar (v.)	*Sit*
Sentir (v.)	*Feel*
Separar (v.)	*Separate*
Sequedad (la) (n.)	*Dryness*
Severo, a (adj.)	*Severe*
Sexo (el) (n.)	*Sex*
Shock (el) (n.)	*Shock*
SIDA (el) (n.)	*AIDS*
Sién (la) (n.)	*Temple*
Sífilis (la) (n.)	*Syphilis*
Silla de ruedas (la) (n.)	*Wheelchair*
Sinápsis (la) (n.)	*Synapses*
Síndrome (el) (n.)	*Syndrome*
Síntoma (el) (n.)	*Symptom*
Sinusitis (la) (n.)	*Sinusitis*
Sistema nervioso (el) (n.)	*Nervous system*
Sobredosis (la) (n.)	*Overdose*
Social (adj.)	*Social*
Sodio (el) (n.)	*Sodium*
Sofocar, asfixiar (v.)	*Suffocate*

Español	Inglés
Solamente (adv.)	*Only*
Solicitud (la) (n.)	*Application*
Solo (adj.)	*Alone*
Soltero, a (adj.)	*Single*
Sordera (la) (n.)	*Deafness*
Sordo, a (adj.)	*Deaf*
Stress (el) (n.)	*Stress*
Subcutáneo, a (adj.)	*Subcutaneous*
Substancia (la) (n.)	*Substance*
Sudar (v.)	*Sweat*
Sudor (el) (n.)	*Sweat*
Suero (el) (n.)	*Serum*
Sufrir (v.)	*Suffer*
Sugerir (v.)	*Suggest*
Suicidarse (v. r.)	*Commit suicide*
Suicidio (el) (n.)	*Suicide*
Supositorio (el) (n.)	*Suppository*
Sutura (la) (n.)	*Suture*
Tabaco (el) (n.)	*Tobacco*
Tablilla (la) (n.)	*Splint*
Talón (el) (n.)	*Heel*
Taquicardia (la) (n.)	*Tachicardia*
Tarjeta (la) (n.)	*Card*
Técnico (el) (n.)	*Technician*
Tejido (el) (n.)	*Tissue*
Temblor (el) (n.)	*Tremors*
Temor (el) (n.)	*Fear*
Temperamento (el) (n.)	*Temperament*
Temperatura (la) (n.)	*Temperature*
Tendencia (la) (n.)	*Tendency*
Tendón de aquiles (el) (n.)	*Achilles tendon*
Tendones (los) (n.)	*Tendons*
Tensión (la) (n.)	*Tension*
Terapia de hormonas (la) (n.)	*Hormone therapy*

Termómetro (el) (n.)	*Thermometer*
Testículos (los) (n.)	*Testicles*
Tétano (el) (n.)	*Tetanus*
Tía (la) (n.)	*Aunt*
Tina (la) (n.)	*Bathtub*
Tiroides (la) (n.)	*Thyroid*
Tobillo (el) (n.)	*Ankle*
Tomar (v.)	*Take*
Tórax (el) (n.)	*Thorax*
Torcedura (la) (n.)	*Twist*
Tos (la) (n.)	*Cough*
Tosferina (la) (n.)	*Whooping cough*
Tóxico, a (adj.)	*Toxic*
Toxinas (las) (n.)	*Toxins*
Tragar (v.)	*Swallow*
Tranquilizante (el) (n.)	*Sedative*
Transfusión (la) (n.)	*Transfusion*
Transmitir (v.)	*Transmit*
Transplante (el) (n.)	*Transplant*
Tráquea (la) (n.)	*Trachea*
Tratamiento (el) (n.)	*Treatment*
Tratar (v.)	*Treat*
Trauma (el) (n.)	*Trauma*
Trompas de Falopio (los) (n.)	*Fallopian Tubes*
Tuberculina (la) (n.)	*Tuberculin*
Tuberculosis (la) (n.)	*Tuberculosis*
Tubo (el) (n.)	*Tube*
Tumor (el) (n.)	*Tumor*
Úlcera (la) (n.)	*Ulcer*
Ultrasonido (el) (n.)	*Ultrasound*
Uña (la) (n.)	*Nail*
Ungüento (el) (n.)	*Ointment*
Uremia (la) (n.)	*Uremia*
Uretra (la) (n.)	*Urethra*

Úrico, a (adj.)	*Uric*
Urólogo (el-la) (n.)	*Urologist*
Urticaria (la) (n.)	*Hives*
Útero (el) (n.)	*Uterus*
Úvula (la) (n.)	*Uvula*
Vacío, a (adj.)	*Empty*
Vacuna (la) (n.)	*Vaccine*
Vagina (la) (n.)	*Vagina*
Vaginitis (la) (n.)	*Vaginitis*
Vaginosis (la) (n.)	*Vaginosis*
Válvula (la) (n.)	*Valve*
Vaporizador (el) (n.)	*Vaporizer*
Varicela (la) (n.)	*Chickenpox*
Várices (las) (n.)	*Varicose veins*
Varón (el) (n.)	*Male*
Vascular (adj.)	*Vascular*
Vasectomía (la) (n.)	*Vasectomy*
Vaselina (la) (n.)	*Vaseline*
Vejiga (la) (n.)	*Bladder*
Vello (el) (n.)	*Body Hair*
Vena (la) (n.)	*Vein*
Venda (la) (n.)	*Bandage*
Veneno (el) (n.)	*Poison*
Venéreo, a (adj.)	*Venereal*
Verdoso, a (adj.)	*Greenish*
Verruga (la) (n.)	*Wart*
Vértebra (la) (n.)	*Vertebra*
Vértigo (el) (n.)	*Vertigo*
Vesícula biliar (la) (n.)	*Gallbladder*
Vida (la) (n.)	*Life*
Viejo (el) (n.)	*Old*
Vino (el) (n.)	*Wine*
Violencia (la) (n.)	*Violence*
Viruela (la) (n.)	*Smallpox*

Virulento, a (adj.)	*Virulent*
Visión (la) (n.)	*Vision*
Visión doble (la) (n.)	*Double vision*
Visita (la) (n.)	*Visit*
Vista fatigada (la) (n.)	*Eyestrain*
Visual (adj.)	*Visual*
Vitamina (la) (n.)	*Vitamin*
Vivir (v.)	*Live*
Vomitar (v.)	*Vomit*
Yeso (el) (n.)	*Cast*
Yodo (el) (n.)	*Iodine*
Zinc (el) (n.)	*Zinc*
Zurdo, a (adj.)	*Left handed*

Vocabulary / Vocabulario

English / Inglés	Spanish / Español
Abnormal	*Anormal (adj.)*
Abortion	*Aborto (el) (n.)*
Abscess	*Absceso (el) (n.)*
Abstinence	*Abstinencia (la) (n.)*
Abuse	*Abuso (el) (n.)*
Accident	*Accidente (el) (n.)*
Ache	*Dolor (el) (n.)*
Achilles tendon	*Tendón de aquiles (el) (n.)*
Acid	*Ácido (el) (n.)*
Acne	*Acné (el) (n.)*
Adam's apple	*Nuez de Adán (la) (n.)*
Addiction	*Adicción (la) (n.)*
Address	*Dirección (la) (n.)*
Adenoids	*Adenoides (la) (n.)*
Adhesive bandage	*Curita (el) (n.)*
Admission	*Admisión (la) (n.)*
Admit	*Internar (v.)*
Adrenaline	*Adrenalina (la) (n.)*
Adults	*Adultos, as (n.)*
Advice	*Consejo (el) (n.)*
Advise	*Aconsejar (v.)*
Aerobic	*Aeróbico (el) (n.)*
Affect	*Afectar (v.)*
Affective	*Afectivo, a (adj.)*
Against	*Contra (prep.)*
Age	*Edad (la) (n.)*
AIDS	*SIDA (el) (n.)*
Air	*Aire (el) (n.)*
Albumin	*Albúmina (la) (n.)*
Alcohol	*Alcohol (el) (n.)*

Alcoholic	*Alcohólico, a (n.) (adj.)*
Alcoholism	*Alcoholismo (el) (n.)*
Allergic	*Alérgico, a (adj.)*
Allergy	*Alergia (la) (n.)*
Alleviate	*Aliviar (v.)*
Alone	*Solo (adj.)*
Alveoli	*Alvéolo (el) (n.)*
Ambulance	*Ambulancia (la) (n.)*
Ambulatory	*Ambulatorio (el) (n.) (adj.)*
Amino acids	*Aminoácidos (los) (n.)*
Amnesia	*Amnesia (la) (n.)*
Amount	*Cantidad (la) (n.)*
Amphetamines	*Anfetaminas (las) (n.)*
Amputate	*Amputar (v.)*
Amputation	*Amputación (la) (n.)*
Anemia	*Anemia (la) (n.)*
Anemic	*Anémico, a (adj.)*
Anesthesia	*Anestesia (la) (n.)*
Anger	*Coraje (el) (n.)*
Ankle	*Tobillo (el) (n.)*
Anorexia	*Anorexia (la) (n.)*
Antacid	*Antiácido (el) (n.) (adj.)*
Antibiotic	*Antibiótico (el) (n.) (adj.)*
Antidote	*Antídoto (el) (n.)*
Antihistamine	*Antiestamínico (el) (n.) (adj.)*
Antinflammatory	*Antiinflamatorio (el) (n.) (adj.)*
Antioxidants	*Antioxidante (n.) (adj.)*
Anus	*Ano (el) (n.)*
Anxiety	*Ansiedad (la) (n.)*
Aorta	*Aorta (la) (n.)*
Appendicitis	*Apendicitis (la) (n.)*
Appendix	*Apéndice (el) (n.)*
Appetite	*Apetito (el) (n.)*
Apple	*Manzana (la) (n.)*

Application	*Solicitud (la) (n.)*
Appointment	*Cita (la) (n.)*
Arm	*Brazo (el) (n.)*
Armpit	*Axila (la) (n.)*
Around	*Alrededor (adv.)*
Arrhythmia	*Arritmia (la) (n.)*
Arrive	*Llegar (v.)*
Arteriosclerosis	*Arteriosclerosis (la) (n.)*
Artery	*Arteria (la) (n.)*
Arthritis	*Artritis (la) (n.)*
Artificial	*Artificial (adj.)*
Ask	*Preguntar (v.)*
Asleep	*Dormido (adj.)*
Asphyxia	*Asfixia (la) (n.)*
Aspirin	*Aspirina (la) (n.)*
Asthma	*Asma (el) (n.)*
Asthmatic	*Asmático, a (adj.)*
Astigmatism	*Astigmatismo (el) (n.)*
Athletes foot	*Pie de atleta (el) (n.)*
Atrophy	*Atrofia (la) (n.)*
Aunt	*Tía (la) (n.)*
Authorization	*Autorización (la) (n.)*
Authorize	*Autorizar (v.)*
Baby	*Bebé (el) (n.)*
Baby bottle	*Mamadera (la) (n.)*
Baby tooth	*Diente de Leche (el) (n.)*
Back	*Espalda (la) (n.)*
Back of the head	*Nuca (la) (n.)*
Back of the knee	*Corva (la) (n.)*
Backwards	*Hacia atrás (adv.)*
Bacteria	*Bacteria (la) (n.)*
Bad	*Malo, a (adj.)*
Balanced	*Balanceado, a (adj.)*
Balloon	*Globo (el) (n.)*

Band aid	*Banda adhesiva (la) (n.)*
Bandage	*Venda (la) (n.)*
Barely	*Apenas (adv.)*
Basic	*Básico, a (adj.)*
Bathe	*Bañar (v.)*
Bathroom	*Baño (el) (n.)*
Bathtub	*Tina (la) (n.)*
Battery	*Batería (la) (n.)*
Beard	*Barba (la) (n.)*
Bed	*Cama (la) (n.)*
Begin	*Empezar (v.)*
Behavior	*Conducta (la) (n.)*
Believe	*Creer (v.)*
Belly	*Abdomen (el) (n.)*
Belly button	*Ombligo (el) (n.)*
Benadryl	*Benadryl (n.)*
Bend	*Doblar (v.)*
Benign	*Benigno, a (adj.)*
Besides	*Además (adv.)*
Better	*Mejor (adj.)*
Bile	*Bilis (la) (n.)*
Bill	*Cuenta (la) (n.)*
Biopsy	*Biopsia (la) (n.)*
Birth	*Nacimiento (el) (n.)*
Birth control	*Control de la natalidad (el) (n.)*
Bite	*Morder (v.)*
Black head	*Espinilla (la) (n.)*
Black heads	*Barros (los) (n.)*
Bladder	*Vejiga (la) (n.)*
Bland	*Blando, a (adj.)*
Blanket	*Cobija (la) (n.)*
Bleach	*Cloro (el) (n.)*
Bleed	*Sangrar (v.)*
Blind	*Ciego, a (adj.)*

Blister	*Ampolla (la) (n.)*
Block	*Cuadra (la) (n.)*
Blood	*Sangre (la) (n.)*
Blood bank	*Banco de sangre (el) (n.)*
Blood pressure	*Presión sanguínea (la) (n.)*
Blood test	*Prueba de sangre (la) (n.)*
Blouse	*Blusa (la) (n.)*
Blurry	*Borroso, a (adj.)*
Body Hair	*Vello (el) (n.)*
Boiling	*Hirviendo (adv.)*
Bone	*Hueso (el) (n.)*
Bone marrow	*Médula ósea (la) (n.)*
Bottle	*Frasco (el) (n.)*
Bowel movement	*Evacuación intestinal (la) (n.)*
Brain	*Cerebro (el) (n.)*
Break	*Romper (v.)*
Breast	*Seno (el) (n.)*
Breast bone	*Esternón (el) (n.)*
Breast feed	*Dar pecho (v.)*
Breath	*Aliento (el) (n.)*
Breathe	*Respirar (v.)*
Bridge	*Puente (el) (n.)*
Bronchitis	*Bronquitis (la) (n.)*
Broth	*Caldo (el) (n.)*
Brother	*Hermano (el) (n.)*
Bruise	*Moretón (el) (n.)*
Building	*Edificio (el) (n.)*
Bulimia	*Bulimia (la) (n.)*
Bunion	*Juanete (el) (n.)*
Burn	*Quemadura (la) (n.)*
Burning	*Ardor (el) (n.)*
Burp	*Eructar (v.)*
Busy	*Ocupado, a (adj.)*
Butter	*Mantequilla (la) (n.)*

Buttocks	*Nalgas (las) (n.)*
Button	*Botón (el) (n.)*
By mouth	*Administración oral (la) (n.)*
Cadaver	*Cadáver (el) (n.)*
Caffeine	*Cafeína (la) (n.)*
Cake	*Pastel (el) (n.)*
Calcium	*Calcio (el) (n.)*
Calf	*Pantorrilla (la) (n.)*
Call	*Llamar (v.)*
Callus	*Callo (el) (n.)*
Calm	*Calma (la) (n.)*
Calorie	*Caloría (la) (n.)*
Camomile	*Manzanilla (la) (n.)*
Cancer	*Cáncer (el) (n.)*
Candy	*Dulce (adj.)*
Canker	*Chancro (el) (n.)*
Capillaries	*Capilares (los) (n.)*
Capsule	*Cápsula (la) (n.)*
Carbohydrate	*Carbohidrato (el) (n.)*
Carcinogenic	*Carcinogénico, a (adj.)*
Card	*Tarjeta (la) (n.)*
Cardiac	*Cardíaco, a (adj.)*
Cardiac arrest	*Paro cardíaco (el) (n.)*
Cardiologist	*Cardiólogo, a (n.)*
Cardiology	*Cardiología (la) (n.)*
Cardiopulmonary	*Cardiopulmonar (adj.)*
Cardiovascular	*Cardiovascular (adj.)*
Care	*Cuidado (el) (n.)*
Cartilage	*Cartílago (el) (n.)*
Case	*Caso (el) (n.)*
Cashier	*Cajero, a (n.)*
Cast	*Yeso (el) (n.)*
Cataracts	*Cataratas (las) (n.)*
Cause	*Causa (la) (n.)*

Cavity	*Carie (la) (n.)*
Cell	*Célula (la) (n.)*
Cerebellum	*Cerebelo (el) (n.)*
Cerebrovascular	*Cerebrovascular (adj.)*
Cervix	*Cerviz (la) (n.)*
Cesarean	*Cesárea (la) (n.)*
Check	*Revisar (v.)*
Check-up	*Examen (el) (n.)*
Chemical	*Químico, a (adj.)*
Chemotherapy	*Quimioterapia (la) (n.)*
Chest	*Pecho (el) (n.)*
Chew	*Masticar (v.)*
Chickenpox	*Varicela (la) (n.)*
Child	*Niño, a (n.) (adj.)*
Chill	*Escalofrío (el) (n.)*
Chin	*Barbilla (la) (n.)*
Choke	*Atragantarse (v. r.)*
Cholesterol	*Colesterol (el) (n.)*
Chromosome	*Cromosoma (el) (n.)*
Chronic	*Crónico, a (adj.)*
Cigarettes	*Cigarros (los) (n.)*
Circulation	*Circulación (la) (n.)*
Circumcision	*Circuncisión (la) (n.)*
Clean	*Limpio, a (adj.)*
Clear	*Claro, a (adj.)*
Clearly	*Claramente (adv.)*
Clinic	*Clínica (la) (n.)*
Clitoris	*Clítoris (el) (n.)*
Clothes	*Ropa (la) (n.)*
Coagulation	*Coagulación (la) (n.)*
Coccyx	*Coxis (el) (n.)*
Coffee	*Café (el) (n.)*
Cognitive	*Cognitivo, a (adj.)*
Cold	*Gripa (la) (n.)*

Colitis	*Colitis (la) (n.)*
Collar Bone	*Clavícula (la) (n.)*
Collide	*Chocar (v.)*
Colon	*Colon (el) (n.)*
Color	*Color (el) (n.)*
Color blind	*Daltonismo (el) (n.)*
Coma	*Coma (el) (n.)*
Come out fine	*Salir bien (v.)*
Comfortable	*Cómodo, a (adj.)*
Commit suicide	*Suicidarse (v. r.)*
Complain	*Quejarse (v. r.)*
Complexion	*Cutis (el) (n.)*
Compulsion	*Compulsión (la) (n.)*
Compulsive	*Compulsivo, a (adj.)*
Conceive	*Concebir (v.)*
Condom	*Condón (el) (n.)*
Confirm	*Confirmar (v.)*
Confusion	*Confusión (la) (n.)*
Congestion	*Congestión (la) (n.)*
Conjunctivitis	*Conjuntivitis (la) (n.)*
Consent	*Consentir (v.)*
Constantly	*Constantemente (adv.)*
Constipation	*Constipación (la) (n.)*
Consult	*Consultar (v.)*
Contact lenses	*Lentes de contacto (los) (n.)*
Contagious	*Contagio (el) (n.)*
Contagious	*Contagioso, a (adj.)*
Contain	*Contener (v.)*
Continue	*Continuar (v.)*
Contraceptive	*Anticonceptivo (el) (n.) (adj.)*
Contraction	*Contracción (la) (n.)*
Control	*Control (el) (n.)*
Contusion	*Contusión (la) (n.)*
Convulsions	*Convulsiones (las) (n.)*

Vocabulary

Cook	*Cocinar (v.)*
Cooked	*Cocinado, a (adj.)*
Coordinator	*Coordinador, a (n.) (adj.)*
Cornea	*Córnea (la) (n.)*
Correct	*Correcto, a (adj.)*
Corticosteroids	*Corticosteroides (los) (n.)*
Cosmetic	*Cosmético (el) (n.) (adj.)*
Cough	*Tos (la) (n.)*
Count	*Contar (v.)*
Couple	*Pareja (la) (n.)*
Cover	*Cubrir (v.)*
Cramp	*Calambre (el) (n.)*
Cramp	*Cólico (el) (n.)*
Cream	*Crema (la) (n.)*
Credential	*Credencial (la) (n.)*
Crib	*Cuna (la) (n.)*
Cross	*Cruz (la) (n.)*
Cross eyed	*Bizco, a (adj.)*
Croup	*Crup (el) (n.)*
Crown	*Corona (la) (n.)*
Crutches	*Muletas (las) (n.)*
Curd	*Grumo (el) (n.)*
Cure	*Cura (la) (n.)*
Currently	*Actualmente (adv.)*
Curtain	*Cortina (la) (n.)*
Cut	*Cortada (la) (n.)*
Cyst	*Quiste (el) (n.)*
Cystitis	*Cistitis (la) (n.)*
Daily	*Diario, a (adj.)*
Dairy	*Lácteo, a (adj.)*
Damage	*Daño (el) (n.)*
Dandruff	*Caspa (la) (n.)*
Dangerous	*Peligroso, a (adj.)*
Dark	*Oscuro, a (adj.)*

Darkness	*Oscuridad (la) (n.)*
Date	*Fecha (la) (n.)*
Daughter	*Hija (la) (n.)*
Deaf	*Sordo, a (adj.)*
Deafness	*Sordera (la) (n.)*
Death	*Muerte (la) (n.)*
Decide	*Decidir (v.)*
Decongestant	*Descongestionante (n.) (adj.)*
Deep	*Hondo, a (adj.)*
Deformity	*Deformidad (la) (n.)*
Degree	*Grado (el) (n.)*
Dehydration	*Deshidratación (la) (n.)*
Delirium	*Delirio (el) (n.)*
Delivery	*Parto (el) (n.)*
Delivery room	*Sala de parto (la) (n.)*
Dementia	*Demencia (la) (n.)*
Dental	*Dental (adj.)*
Dental-floss	*Hilo dental (el) (n.)*
Dentist	*Dentista (el-la) (n.)*
Dentures	*Dentadura (la) (n.)*
Department	*Departamento (el) (n.)*
Depression	*Depresión (la) (n.)*
Dermatitis	*Dermatitis (la) (n.)*
Dermatologist	*Dermatólogo (el-la) (n.)*
Destroy	*Destruir (v.)*
Detachment	*Desprendimiento (el) (n.)*
Detergent	*Detergente (el) (n.)*
Determine	*Determinar (v.)*
Detox	*Desintoxicación (la) (n.)*
Diabetes	*Diabetes (la) (n.)*
Diabetic	*Diabético, a (n.) (adj.)*
Diagnosis	*Diagnosis (la) (n.)*
Diagnostic	*Diagnóstico (el) (n.)*
Dialysis	*Diálisis (la) (n.)*

Diapers	*Pañales (los) (n.)*
Diaphragm	*Diafragma (el) (n.)*
Diarrhea	*Diarrea (la) (n.)*
Diet	*Dieta (la) (n.)*
Dietitian	*Dietista (n.)*
Different	*Diferente (adj.)*
Difficult	*Difícil (adj.)*
Difficulty	*Dificultad (la) (n.)*
Digest	*Digerir (v.)*
Digestive	*Digestivo (el) (n.)*
Dilated	*Dilatado, a (adj.)*
Diminish	*Disminuir (v.)*
Diphtheria	*Difteria (la) (n.)*
Disability	*Incapacidad (la) (n.)*
Disaster	*Desastre (el) (n.)*
Discharge	*Dar de alta (v.)*
Discharge	*Secreción (la) (n.)*
Discipline	*Disciplina (la) (n.)*
Discomfort	*Malestar (el) (n.)*
Disinfect	*Desinfectar (v.)*
Disk	*Disco (el) (n.)*
Dislocation	*Dislocación (la) (n.)*
Dizziness	*Mareo (el) (n.)*
Doctor	*Doctor, ra (n.)*
Doctor, MD	*Médico (el) (n.)*
Doctor's office	*Consultorio (el) (n.)*
Domestic	*Doméstico, a (adj.)*
Dominant	*Dominante (adj.)*
Dorsal	*Dorsal (adj.)*
Dorsal spine	*Espina dorsal (la) (n.)*
Dosage	*Dosis (la) (n.)*
Double vision	*Visión doble (la) (n.)*
Downward	*Hacia abajo (adv.)*
Drink	*Beber (v.)*

Dropper	*Gotero (el) (n.)*
Drops	*Gotas (las) (n.)*
Drug	*Droga (la) (n.)*
Drug addict	*Drogadicto, a (n.) (adj.)*
Dry	*Seco, a (adj.)*
Dryness	*Sequedad (la) (n.)*
Duodenum	*Duodeno (el) (n.)*
Ear	*Oído (el) (n.)*
Earwax	*Cerilla (la) (n.)*
Eat	*Comer (v.)*
Eczema	*Eczema (el) (n.)*
Edema	*Edema (el) (n.)*
Effective	*Efectivo, a (adj.)*
Effort	*Esfuerzo (el) (n.)*
Egg	*Huevo (el) (n.)*
Ejaculation	*Eyaculación (la) (n.)*
Elbow	*Codo (el) (n.)*
Elderly man	*Anciano (el) (n.)*
Elderly woman	*Anciana (la) (n.)*
Electric	*Eléctrico, a (adj.)*
Electrocardiogram, EKG	*Electrocardiograma (el) (n.)*
Elevator	*Elevador (el) (n.)*
Emergency	*Emergencia (la) (n.)*
Emphysema	*Enfisema (el) (n.)*
Empty	*Vacío, a (adj.)*
Encephalitis	*Encefalitis (la) (n.)*
Encopresis	*Encopresis (la) (n.)*
Endocrinologist	*Endocrinólogo (el-la) (n.)*
Endoscope	*Endoscopio (el) (n.)*
Endoscopy	*Endoscopía (la) (n.)*
Enema	*Enema (la) (n.)*
Entrance	*Entrada (la) (n.)*
Enuresis	*Enuresis (la) (n.)*
Enzyme	*Enzima (la) (n.)*

Epidermis	*Epidermis (la) (n.)*
Epilepsy	*Epilepsia (la) (n.)*
Epinephrine	*Epinefrina (la) (n.)*
Equipment	*Equipo (el) (n.)*
Erection	*Erección (la) (n.)*
Esophagus	*Esófago (el) (n.)*
Estrogen	*Estrógeno (el) (n.)*
Exercise	*Ejercicio (el) (n.)*
Exhaust	*Exhausto, a (adj.)*
Exhausted	*Agotado, a (adj.)*
Expectorant	*Expectorante (adj.)*
Extract	*Extraer (v.)*
Eye	*Ojo (el) (n.)*
Eye glasses	*Gafas (las) (n.)*
Eyebrows	*Cejas (las) (n.)*
Eyelash	*Pestaña (la) (n.)*
Eyelid	*Párpado (el) (n.)*
Eyestrain	*Vista fatigada (la) (n.)*
Face	*Cara (la) (n.)*
Face down	*Boca abajo (adv.)*
Face up	*Boca arriba (adv.)*
Factors	*Factores (los) (n.)*
Faint	*Desmayo (el) (n.)*
Faithfully	*Fielmente (adv.)*
Fall	*Caer (v.)*
Fallopian Tubes	*Trompas de Falopio (los) (n.)*
Family	*Familia (la) (n.)*
Far	*Lejos (adv.)*
Fast	*Ayunar (v.)*
Fat	*Grasa (la) (n.)*
Father	*Padre (el) (n.)*
Fatigue	*Fatiga (la) (n.)*
Fear	*Miedo (el) (n.)*
Fear	*Temor (el) (n.)*

Feces	*Heces (las) (n.)*
Feel	*Sentir (v.)*
Femur	*Fémur (el) (n.)*
Fertile	*Fértil (adj.)*
Fetus	*Feto (el) (n.)*
Fever	*Fiebre (la) (n.)*
Fiber	*Fibra (la) (n.)*
File	*Archivo (el) (n.)*
Fill out	*Llenar (v.)*
Finally	*Finalmente (adv.)*
Finger	*Dedo (el) (n.)*
First aid	*Primeros auxilios (los) (n.)*
Fish	*Pescado (el) (n.)*
Fluoroscopy	*Fluoroscopía (la) (n.)*
Foam	*Espuma (la) (n.)*
Fontanelle	*Fontanela (la) (n.)*
Food	*Comida (la) (n.)*
Foot	*Pie (el) (n.)*
Forceps	*Fórceps (el) (n.)*
Forehead	*Frente (la) (n.)*
Form	*Forma (la) (n.)*
Formula	*Fórmula (la) (n.)*
Forward	*Hacia adelante (adv.)*
Fracture	*Fractura (la) (n.)*
Frequently	*Frecuente (adv.)*
Friction	*Fricción (la) (n.)*
Frigidity	*Frigidez (la) (n.)*
From	*Desde (prep.)*
Gallbladder	*Vesícula biliar (la) (n.)*
Gamma globulin	*Gamaglobulina (la) (n.)*
Ganglion	*Ganglio (el) (n.)*
Gangrene	*Gangrena (la) (n.)*
Gargle	*Gárgaras (las) (n.)*
Gas	*Gas (el) (n.)*

Gastric	*Gástrico, a (adj.)*
Gastritis	*Gastritis (la) (n.)*
Gastroenteritis	*Gastroenteritis (la) (n.)*
Gastrointestinal	*Gastrointestinal (adj.)*
Gauze	*Gasa (la) (n.)*
Gene	*Gene (el) (n.)*
General	*General (el) (n.)*
Genetic	*Genético, a (adj.)*
Genital	*Genital (adj.)*
Genitals	*Genitales (los) (n.)*
Geriatric	*Geriatra (el-la) (n.)*
Germ	*Germen (el) (n.)*
Gestation	*Gestación (la) (n.)*
Gingivitis	*Gingivitis (la) (n.)*
Give birth	*Parir (v.)*
Gland	*Glándula (la) (n.)*
Glasses	*Anteojos (los) (n.)*
Glaucoma	*Glaucoma (el) (n.)*
Globulin	*Globulina (la) (n.)*
Glucose	*Glucosa (la) (n.)*
Goiter	*Bocio (el) (n.)*
Gonorrhea	*Gonorrea (la) (n.)*
Gout	*Gota (la) (n.)*
Grandfather	*Abuelo (el) (n.)*
Grandmother	*Abuela (la) (n.)*
Greenish	*Verdoso, a (adj.)*
Grief	*Duelo (el) (n.)*
Groin	*Entrepierna (la) (n.)*
Group	*Grupo (el) (n.)*
Guerney	*Camilla (la) (n.)*
Gum	*Encía (la) (n.)*
Gynecologist	*Ginecólogo (el-la) (n.)*
Habits	*Hábitos (los) (n.)*
Hair	*Pelo (el) (n.)*

Half	*Mitad (la) (n.)*
Halitosis	*Halitosis (la) (n.)*
Hallucination	*Alucinación (la) (n.)*
Hallway	*Pasillo (el) (n.)*
Hand	*Mano (la) (n.)*
Hard	*Duro (adj.)*
Hardening	*Endurecimiento (el) (n.)*
Hay fever	*Fiebre de heno (la) (n.)*
Head	*Cabeza (la) (n.)*
Head ache	*Dolor de cabeza (el) (n.)*
Health	*Salud (la) (n.)*
Healthy	*Sano, a (adj.)*
Hearing aid	*Audífono (el) (n.)*
Heart	*Corazón (el) (n.)*
Heart attack	*Infarto (el) (n.)*
Heart beat	*Latido (el) (n.)*
Heart rhythm	*Ritmo cardíaco (el) (n.)*
Heartburn	*Agrura (la) (n.)*
Heavy	*Pesado, a (adj.)*
Heel	*Talón (el) (n.)*
Help	*Ayudar (v.)*
Hematoma	*Hematoma (el) (n.)*
Hemiplegia	*Hemiplejía (la) (n.)*
Hemoglobin	*Hemoglobina (la) (n.)*
Hemorrhage	*Hemorragia (la) (n.)*
Hemorrhoids	*Hemorroides (las) (n.)*
Hepatic	*Hepático, a (adj.)*
Hepatitis	*Hepatitis (la) (n.)*
Hereditary	*Hereditario, a (adj.)*
Hernia	*Hernia (la) (n.)*
Herpes	*Herpes (el) (n.)*
Hiccups	*Hipo (el) (n.)*
High	*Alto, a (adj.)*
Hip	*Cadera (la) (n.)*

Hit	*Golpear (v.)*
Hives	*Urticaria (la) (n.)*
Hoarse	*Ronco, a (adj.)*
Hoarseness	*Ronquera (la) (n.)*
Hole	*Agujero (el) (n.)*
Home remedy	*Remedio casero (el) (n.)*
Honey	*Miel (la) (n.)*
Hormone	*Hormona (la) (n.)*
Hormone therapy	*Terapia de hormonas (la) (n.)*
Hospital	*Hospital (el) (n.)*
Hot flashes	*Bochornos (los) (n.)*
Hurt	*Lastimar (v.)*
Husband	*Esposo (el) (n.)*
Hyperactive	*Hiperactivo, a (adj.)*
Hyperglycemia	*Hiperglucemia (la) (n.)*
Hypertension	*Hipertensión (la) (n.)*
Hyperventilation	*Hiperventilación (la) (n.)*
Hypochondria	*Hipocondría (la) (n.)*
Hypothalamus	*Hipotálamo (el) (n.)*
Hypothermia	*Hipotermia (la) (n.)*
Hysterectomy	*Histerectomía (la) (n.)*
Ibuprofen	*Ibuprofen (el) (n.)*
Ice	*Hielo (el) (n.)*
Iced	*Helado (el) (n.)*
Idiopathic	*Ideopático, a (adj.)*
Immediately	*Inmediatamente (adv.)*
Immobilize	*Inmovilizar (v.)*
Immune	*Inmune (adj.)*
Immunization	*Inmunización (la) (n.)*
Immunology	*Inmunológico, a (adj.)*
Immunotherapy	*Inmunoterápia (la) (n.)*
Impetigo	*Impétigo (el) (n.)*
Important	*Importante (adv.)*
Impotence	*Impotencia (la) (n.)*

Improve	*Mejorar (v.)*
Inch	*Pulgada (la) (n.)*
Incision	*Incisión (la) (n.)*
Incontinence	*Incontinencia (la) (n.)*
Increase	*Aumentar (v.)*
Incubation	*Incubación (la) (n.)*
Incubator	*Incubador (el) (n.)*
Index finger	*Indice (el) (n.)*
Indicate	*Indicar (v.)*
Indication	*Indicación (la) (n.)*
Indigestion	*Indigestión (la) (n.)*
Infect	*Infectar (v.)*
Infection	*Infección (la) (n.)*
Infectious	*Infeccioso, a (adj.)*
Infertile	*Infértil (adj.)*
Inhaler	*Inhalador (el) (n.)*
Inject	*Inyectar (v.)*
Injection	*Inyección (la) (n.)*
Injured Person	*Herido, a (n.) (adj.)*
Injury	*Herida (la) (n.)*
Insanity	*Locura (la) (n.)*
Insecticide	*Insecticida (el) (n.)*
Insects	*Insectos (los) (n.)*
Insemination	*Inseminación (la) (n.)*
Insert	*Insertar (v.)*
Inside	*Adentro (adv.)*
Insomnia	*Insomnio (el) (n.)*
Instruction	*Instrucción (la) (n.)*
Insulin	*Insulina (la) (n.)*
Insurance	*Seguro (el) (n.)*
Insurance company	*Compañía de seguros (la) (n.)*
Intensive	*Intensivo, a (adj.)*
Intensive care	*Cuidados Intensivos (los) (n.)*
Interaction	*Interacción (la) (n.)*

Intercourse	*Acto sexual (el) (n.)*
Intestines	*Intestinos (los) (n.)*
Intolerance	*Intolerancia (la) (n.)*
Intoxication	*Intoxicación (la) (n.)*
Intravenous	*Intravenoso, a (adj.)*
Iodine	*Yodo (el) (n.)*
Iris	*Iris (el) (n.)*
Irregular	*Irregular (adj.)*
Irritation	*Irritación (la) (n.)*
Itch	*Comezón (la) (n.)*
IUD	*Dispositivo intrauterino (el) (n.)*
Jacket	*Chaqueta (la) (n.)*
Jaw	*Mandíbula (la) (n.)*
Jaw	*Quijada (la) (n.)*
Jelly	*Jalea (la) (n.)*
Joint	*Articulación (la) (n.)*
Joint	*Coyuntura (la) (n.)*
Juice	*Jugo (el) (n.)*
Kaopectate	*Kaopectate (el) (n.)*
Kidney	*Riñón (el) (n.)*
Knee	*Rodilla (la) (n.)*
Know	*Conocer (v.)*
Knuckle	*Nudillo (el) (n.)*
Labor	*Parto (el) (n.)*
Labor pains	*Dolores de parto (los) (n.)*
Laboratory	*Laboratorio (el) (n.)*
Laceration	*Laceración (la) (n.)*
Lachrymal gland	*Glándula lagrimal (la) (n.)*
Large	*Grande (adj.)*
Laryngitis	*Laringitis (la) (n.)*
Larynx	*Laringe (la) (n.)*
Last name	*Apellido (el) (n.)*
Laxative	*Laxante (adj.)*
Left	*Izquierdo, a (adj.)*

Left handed	*Zurdo, a (adj.)*
Leg	*Pierna (la) (n.)*
Lesion	*Lesión (la) (n.)*
Lethargic	*Letargo (el) (n.)*
Leukemia	*Leucemia (la) (n.)*
Libido	*Líbido (la) (n.)*
Lice	*Piojos (los) (n.)*
Life	*Vida (la) (n.)*
Ligament	*Ligamento (el) (n.)*
Light	*Ligero, a (adj.)*
Limbs	*Extremidades (las) (n.)*
Limitation	*Limitación (la) (n.)*
Lip	*Labio (el) (n.)*
Liposuction	*Liposucción (la) (n.)*
Lips	*Labios (los) (n.)*
Liquid	*Líquido (el) (n.)*
List	*Lista (la) (n.)*
Live	*Vivir (v.)*
Liver	*Hígado (el) (n.)*
Local	*Local (adj.)*
Localized	*Localizado, a (adj.)*
Look	*Mirar (v.)*
Lose weight	*Adelgazar (v.)*
Loss	*Pérdida (la) (n.)*
Lotion	*Loción (la) (n.)*
Lower back	*Lumbar (adj.)*
Lubricate	*Lubricar (v.)*
Lump	*Bola (la) (n.)*
Lunch	*Almorzar (v.)*
Lung	*Pulmón (el) (n.)*
Lying down	*Acostado, a (adj.)*
Lymph node	*Ganglio linfático (el) (n.)*
Lymphatic	*Linfático, a (adj.)*
Lymphatic nodes	*Nudos linfáticos (los) (n.)*

Magnesia	*Magnesia (la) (n.)*
Make up	*Maquillaje (el) (n.)*
Male	*Varón (el) (n.)*
Malignant	*Maligno, a (adj.)*
Mammogram	*Mamograma (el) (n.)*
Man	*Hombre (el) (n.)*
Mania	*Manía (la) (n.)*
Manner	*Manera (la) (n.)*
Married	*Casado, a (adj.)*
Massage	*Masaje (el) (n.)*
Maternity ward	*Sala de maternidad (la) (n.)*
Measles	*Sarampión (el) (n.)*
Measure	*Medir (v.)*
Medical chart	*Expediente médico (el) (n.)*
Medical report	*Reporte médico (el) (n.)*
Medical-history	*Historia clínica (la) (n.)*
Medications	*Medicamentos (los) (n.)*
Medicine	*Medicina (la) (n.)*
Medicine chest	*Botiquín (el) (n.)*
Medulla	*Médula (la) (n.)*
Melanoma	*Melanoma (el) (n.)*
Membrane	*Membrana (la) (n.)*
Meningitis	*Meningitis (la) (n.)*
Menopause	*Menopausia (la) (n.)*
Menstruation	*Menstruación (la) (n.)*
Mental	*Mental (adj.)*
Mental health	*Salud mental (la) (n.)*
Mental illness	*Enfermedad mental (la) (n.)*
Mercurochrome	*Mercurocromo (el) (n.)*
Metabolism	*Metabolismo (el) (n.)*
Method	*Método (el) (n.)*
Microbes	*Microbios (los) (n.)*
Middle	*Medio (el) (n.)*
Midnight	*Medianoche (la) (n.)*

Midwife	*Partera (la) (n.)*
Migraine	*Migraña (la) (n.)*
Milk	*Leche (la) (n.)*
Mineral	*Mineral (el) (n.)*
Minor	*Menor (adj.)*
Miscarriage	*Malparto (el) (n.)*
Moderate	*Moderado, a (adj.)*
Molar	*Muela (la) (n.)*
Mole	*Lunar (el) (n.)*
Mononucleosis	*Mononucleosis (la) (n.)*
Month	*Mes (el) (n.)*
Mosquito	*Mosquito (el) (n.)*
Mother	*Mamá (la) (n.)*
Mouth	*Boca (la) (n.)*
Mucous	*Moco (el) (n.)*
Mucous membrane	*Mucosa (la) (n.)*
Mumps	*Paperas (las) (n.)*
Muscle	*Músculo (el) (n.)*
Mustache	*Bigote (el) (n.)*
Nail	*Uña (la) (n.)*
Name	*Nombre (el) (n.)*
Narrow	*Estrecho, a (adj.)*
Nasal	*Nasal (adj.)*
Nasal canal	*Canal en la naríz (el) (n.)*
Native	*Natal (adj.)*
Natural	*Natural (adj.)*
Nausea	*Náusea (la) (n.)*
Near sighted	*Miope (n.) (adj.)*
Necessary	*Necesario, a (adj.)*
Neck	*Cuello (el) (n.)*
Need	*Necesitar (v.)*
Needle	*Aguja (la) (n.)*
Negative	*Negativo, a (adj.)*
Neonate	*Neonato (el) (n.)*

Nerve	*Nervio (el) (n.)*
Nervous	*Nervioso, a (adj.)*
Nervous system	*Sistema nerviosos (el) (n.)*
Neuralgia	*Neuralgia (la) (n.)*
Neurologist	*Neurólogo (el-la) (n.)*
Neuron	*Neurona (la) (n.)*
Neurotransmitters	*Neurotransmisores (los) (n.)*
Newborn	*Recién nacido, a (n.) (adj.)*
Nicotine	*Nicotina (la) (n.)*
Night	*Noche (la) (n.)*
Nightmare	*Pesadilla (la) (n.)*
Nipple	*Pezón (el) (n.)*
Noise	*Ruido (el) (n.)*
Non fat milk	*Leche descremada (la) (n.)*
Normal	*Normal (adj.)*
Normally	*Normalmente (adv.)*
Nose	*Nariz (la) (n.)*
Nose drops	*Gotas para la nariz (las) (n.)*
Nostril	*Fosas nasales (las) (n.)*
Notice	*Notar (v.)*
Nourishment	*Alimento (el) (n.)*
Novocain	*Novocaína (la) (n.)*
Now	*Ahora (adv.)*
Nuclear	*Núcleo (el) (n.)*
Numb	*Entumecido, a (adj.)*
Nurse	*Enfermera (la) (n.)*
Nursing department	*Enfermería (la) (n.)*
Nutrition	*Nutrición (la) (n.)*
Obesity	*Obesidad (la) (n.)*
Object	*Objeto (el) (n.)*
Obstructed	*Obstruido, a (adj.)*
Occipital	*Occipital (adj.)*
Occupation	*Ocupación (la) (n.)*
Ocular	*Ocular (adj.)*

Oculist	*Oculista (el-la) (n.)*
Odor	*Olor (el) (n.)*
Office	*Oficina (la) (n.)*
Oil	*Aceite (el) (n.)*
Oily	*Grasoso, a (adj.)*
Ointment	*Ungüento (el) (n.)*
Old	*Viejo (el) (n.)*
Olfactory	*Olfatorio, a (adj.)*
Oncologist	*Oncólogo (el-la) (n.)*
Only	*Solamente (adv.)*
Operate	*Operar (v.)*
Operation	*Operación (la) (n.)*
Ophthalmologist	*Oftalmólogo (el-la) (n.)*
Optical	*Óptico, a (adj.)*
Optimism	*Optimismo (el) (n.)*
Optometrist	*Optométrico, a (adj.)*
Oral	*Oral (adj.)*
Orbit	*Órbita (la) (n.)*
Organ	*Órgano (el) (n.)*
Orgasm	*Orgasmo (el) (n.)*
Orthodontics	*Ortodoncia (la) (n.)*
Orthodontist	*Ortodoncista (el-la) (n.)*
Orthopedics	*Ortopedia (la) (n.)*
Orthopedist	*Ortopedista (el-la) (n.)*
Osteoporosis	*Osteoporosis (la) (n.)*
Outpatient	*Paciente externo (el, la) (n.)*
Ovary	*Ovario (el) (n.)*
Overdose	*Sobredosis (la) (n.)*
Overweight	*Exceso de peso (el) (n.)*
Ovulation	*Ovulación (la) (n.)*
Oxygen	*Oxígeno (el) (n.)*
Pacemaker	*Marcapaso (el) (n.)*
Pack of cigarettes	*Cajetilla (la) (n.)*
Painful	*Doloroso, a (adj.)*

English	Spanish
Palate	*Paladar (el) (n.)*
Pale	*Pálido, a (adj.)*
Palpitations	*Palpitaciones (las) (n.)*
Pamphlet	*Folleto (el) (n.)*
Pancreas	*Páncreas (el) (n.)*
Panic	*Pánico (el) (n.)*
Pap smear test	*Examen vaginal (el) (n.)*
Paper	*Papel (el) (n.)*
Paralysis	*Parálisis (la) (n.)*
Paramedic	*Paramédico (el) (n.)*
Paranoia	*Paranoia (la) (n.)*
Paraplegia	*Paraplejía (la) (n.)*
Parasite	*Parásito (el) (n.)*
Parents	*Padres (los) (n.)*
Partial	*Parcial (adj.)*
Pathogenic	*Patógeno, a (adj.)*
Pathological	*Patológico, a (adj.)*
Pathology	*Patología (la) (n.)*
Patient	*Paciente (el) (n.)*
Pay	*Pagar (v.)*
Payment	*Pago (el) (n.)*
Pedialyte	*Pedialyte (el) (n.)*
Pediatrician	*Pediatra (el-la) (n.)*
Pelvis	*Pelvis (la) (n.)*
Penicillin	*Penicilina (la) (n.)*
Penis	*Pene (el) (n.)*
Perfume	*Perfume (el) (n.)*
Pericardium	*Pericardio (el) (n.)*
Period	*Período (el) (n.)*
Peritonitis	*Peritonitis (la) (n.)*
Peroxide	*Peróxido (el) (n.)*
Persistent	*Persistente (adj.)*
Person	*Persona (la) (n.)*
Pessimism	*Pesimismo (el) (n.)*

Pharmacy	*Farmacia (la) (n.)*
Phobia	*Fobia (la) (n.)*
Physical	*Físico, a (adj.)*
Physiotherapy	*Fisioterapia (la) (n.)*
Pigment	*Pigmento (el) (n.)*
Pill	*Pastilla (la) (n.)*
Pillow	*Almohada (la) (n.)*
Pimple	*Grano (el) (n.)*
Pinch	*Piquete (el) (n.)*
Pit of Stomach	*Epigastrio (el) (n.)*
Pituitary gland	*Glándula pituitaria (la) (n.)*
Placebo	*Placebo (el) (n.)*
Placenta	*Placenta (la) (n.)*
Plague	*Plaga (la) (n.)*
Planning	*Planificación (la) (n.)*
Plaque	*Sarro (el) (n.)*
Plasma	*Plasma (el) (n.)*
Pneumonia	*Pulmonía (la) (n.)*
Poison	*Veneno (el) (n.)*
Poisoning	*Envenenamiento (el) (n.)*
Policy	*Póliza (la) (n.)*
Polio	*Poliomielitis (la) (n.)*
Polite	*Amable (adj.)*
Pollen	*Polen (el) (n.)*
Pores	*Poros (los) (n.)*
Portion	*Porción (la) (n.)*
Positive	*Positivo, a (adj.)*
Postpartum	*Postparto (el) (n.)*
Posture	*Postura (la) (n.)*
Potassium	*Potasio (el) (n.)*
Pound	*Libra (la) (n.)*
Precaution	*Precaución (la) (n.)*
Pregnancy	*Embarazo (el) (n.)*
Pregnant	*Embarazada (la) (adj.)*

Premature	*Prematuro, a (adj.)*
Preparation	*Preparación (la) (n.)*
Prescribe	*Recetar (v.)*
Prescription	*Prescripción (la) (n.)*
Preservatives	*Preservativos (los) (n.)*
Pressure	*Presión (la) (n.)*
Prevention	*Prevención (la) (n.)*
Prick	*Pinchar (v.)*
Primary	*Primario, a (adj.)*
Problem	*Problema (el) (n.)*
Progesterone	*Progesterona (la) (n.)*
Prognosis	*Pronóstico (el) (n.)*
Prophylactic	*Profiláctico, a (adj.)*
Prostate gland	*Próstata (la) (n.)*
Protection	*Protección (la) (n.)*
Protein	*Proteína (la) (n.)*
Psychiatrist	*Psiquiatra (el-la) (n.)*
Psychiatry	*Psiquiatría (la) (n.)*
Psychologist	*Psicólogo (el-la) (n.)*
Psychology	*Psicología (la) (n.)*
Psychometric	*Psicométrico, a (adj.)*
Psychomotor	*Psicomotor, ra (adj.)*
Psychosis	*Psicosis (la) (n.)*
Psychosomatic	*Psicosomático, a (adj.)*
Psychotherapy	*Psicoterapia (la) (n.)*
Puberty	*Pubertad (la) (n.)*
Pubic area	*Pubis (el) (n.)*
Pulse	*Pulso (el) (n.)*
Pupil	*Pupila (la) (n.)*
Pus	*Pus (el) (n.)*
Push	*Empujar (v.)*
Quadriplegic	*Cuadriplegia (la) (n.)*
Rabies	*Rabia (la) (n.)*
Radiation	*Radiación (la) (n.)*

Radiologist	*Radiólogo (el-la) (n.)*
Raise	*Levantar (v.)*
Rash	*Salpullido (el) (n.)*
Reaction	*Reacción (la) (n.)*
Receptionist	*Recepcionista (el-la) (n.)*
Recessive	*Recesivo, a (adj.)*
Recommend	*Recomendar (v.)*
Rectum	*Recto (el) (n.)*
Recurrent	*Recurrente (adj.)*
Reflex	*Reflejo (el) (n.)*
Regular	*Regular (adj.)*
Regularly	*Regularmente (adv.)*
Rehydration	*Rehidratación (la) (n.)*
Relapse	*Recaída (la) (n.)*
Relative	*Pariente (el) (n.)*
Relax	*Relajarse (v. r.)*
Relaxation	*Relajación (la) (n.)*
Relief	*Alivio (el) (n.)*
Remedy	*Remedio (el) (n.)*
Remission	*Remisión (la) (n.)*
Renal	*Renal (adj.)*
Repellent	*Repelentes (los) (n.)*
Report	*Informe (el) (n.)*
Rescue	*Rescate (el) (n.)*
Respiratory	*Respiratorio (el) (n.)*
Rest	*Descanso (el) (n.)*
Result	*Resultado (el) (n.)*
Retina	*Retina (la) (n.)*
Return	*Regresar (v.)*
Rheumatic fever	*Fiebre reumática (la) (n.)*
Rheumatism	*Reumatismo (el) (n.)*
Rheumatologist	*Reumatólogo (el-la) (n.)*
Rhythm	*Ritmo (el) (n.)*
Rib	*Costilla (la) (n.)*

English	Spanish
Right	*Derecho (el) (n.)*
Right handed	*Diestro, a (adj.)*
Risk	*Riesgo (el) (n.)*
Robe	*Bata (la) (n.)*
Root	*Raíz (la) (n.)*
Rubella	*Rubeola (la) (n.)*
Rupture	*Ruptura (la) (n.)*
Saliva	*Saliva (la) (n.)*
Salt	*Sal (la) (n.)*
Sample	*Muestra (la) (n.)*
Save	*Salvar (v.)*
Scab	*Costra (la) (n.)*
Scabies	*Sarna (la) (n.)*
Scalp	*Cuero cabelludo (el) (n.)*
Scar	*Cicatriz (la) (n.)*
Scared	*Asustarse (v. r.)*
Scarlet fever	*Fiebre escarlatina (la) (n.)*
Scrape	*Raspadura (la) (n.)*
Scratch	*Rasguño (el) (n.)*
Scrotum	*Escroto (el) (n.)*
Second opinion	*Segunda opinión (la) (n.)*
Secondary	*Secundario, a (adj.)*
Secretary	*Secretario (el) (n.)*
Sedative	*Tranquilizante (el) (n.)*
Seizure	*Ataque (el) (n.)*
Self exam	*Auto examen (el) (n.)*
Semen	*Semen (el) (n.)*
Separate	*Separar (v.)*
Serious	*Grave (adj.)*
Serum	*Suero (el) (n.)*
Severe	*Severo, a (adj.)*
Sex	*Sexo (el) (n.)*
Sexual abuse	*Abuso sexual (el) (n.)*
Sexual intercourse	*Relación sexual (la) (n.)*

Sexual partner	*Compañero, a sexual (n.)*
Sharp	*Agudo, a (adj.)*
Sharp pain	*Punzada (la) (n.)*
Shave	*Rasurar (v.)*
Shin of leg	*Espinilla (la) (n.)*
Shock	*Shock (el) (n.)*
Shoulder	*Hombro (el) (n.)*
Shoulder blade	*Escápula (la) (n.)*
Sick	*Enfermo, a (n.)*
Sickness	*Enfermedad (la) (n.)*
Side	*Lado (el) (n.)*
Side effect	*Efecto colateral (el) (n.)*
Signature	*Firma (la) (n.)*
Single	*Soltero, a (adj.)*
Sinus	*Cavidad nasal (la) (n.)*
Sinusitis	*Sinusitis (la) (n.)*
Sister	*Hermana (la) (n.)*
Sit	*Sentar (v.)*
Skeletal muscles	*Musculoesquelético (el) (n.)*
Skeleton	*Esqueleto (el) (n.)*
Skin	*Piel (la) (n.)*
Skull	*Cráneo (el) (n.)*
Sleep	*Dormir (v.)*
Slow	*Lento, a (adj.)*
Slowly	*Lentamente (adv.)*
Smallpox	*Viruela (la) (n.)*
Smoke	*Fumar (v.)*
Soap	*Jabón (el) (n.)*
Social	*Social (adj.)*
Social security	*Seguro social (el) (n.)*
Sodium	*Sodio (el) (n.)*
Sole	*Planta del pie (la) (n.)*
Some	*Algunos, as (adj.)*
Something	*Algo (pron.)*

Sometimes	*Algunas veces (adj.)*
Son	*Hijo (el) (n.)*
Sore	*Llaga (la) (n.)*
Sore throat	*Dolor de garganta (el) (n.)*
Spasm	*Espasmo (el) (n.)*
Specialty	*Especialidad (la) (n.)*
Spermicide	*Espermicida (el) (n.) (adj.)*
Spicy	*Condimentado, a (adj.)*
Spinal anesthesia	*Raquianestesia (la) (n.)*
Spine	*Columna vertebral (la) (n.)*
Spirituality	*Espiritualidad (la) (n.)*
Spit	*Escupir (v.)*
Spleen	*Bazo (el) (n.)*
Splint	*Tablilla (la) (n.)*
Sponge	*Esponja (la) (n.)*
Spoonful	*Cucharada (la) (n.)*
Sputum	*Flema (la) (n.)*
Squeeze	*Apretar (v.)*
Stand	*Aguantar (v.)*
Sterility	*Esterilidad (la) (n.)*
Sterilization	*Esterilización (la) (n.)*
Steroids	*Esteroides (los) (adj.)*
Stethoscope	*Estetoscopio (el) (n.)*
Stitch	*Punto (el) (n.)*
Stomach	*Estómago (el) (n.)*
Stool	*Excremento (el) (n.)*
Stress	*Stress (el) (n.)*
Stroke	*Embolia (la) (n.)*
Study	*Estudio (el) (n.)*
Stupor	*Estupor (el) (n.)*
Sty	*Orzuelo (el) (n.)*
Subcutaneous	*Subcutáneo, a (adj.)*
Substance	*Substancia (la) (n.)*
Sudden	*Repentino, a (adj.)*

Suffer	*Sufrir (v.)*
Suffocate	*Sofocar, asfixiar (v.)*
Suggest	*Sugerir (v.)*
Suicide	*Suicidio (el) (n.)*
Summary	*Resumen (el) (n.)*
Sunstroke	*Insolación (la) (n.)*
Suppository	*Supositorio (el) (n.)*
Surgeon	*Cirujano (el) (n.)*
Surgery	*Cirugía (la) (n.)*
Surgical intervention	*Intervención (la) (n.)*
Suture	*Sutura (la) (n.)*
Swallow	*Tragar (v.)*
Sweat	*Sudar (v.)*
Sweat	*Sudor (el) (n.)*
Swollen	*Inflamado, a (adj.)*
Symptom	*Síntoma (el) (n.)*
Synapses	*Sinapsis (la) (n.)*
Syndrome	*Síndrome (el) (n.)*
Syphilis	*Sífilis (la) (n.)*
Syrup	*Jarabe (el) (n.)*
Tachicardia	*Taquicardia (la) (n.)*
Take	*Tomar (v.)*
Technician	*Técnico (el) (n.)*
Temper tantrum	*Berrinche (el) (n.)*
Temperament	*Temperamento (el) (n.)*
Temperature	*Temperatura (la) (n.)*
Temple	*Sien (la) (n.)*
Tendency	*Tendencia (la) (n.)*
Tendons	*Tendones (los) (n.)*
Tension	*Tensión (la) (n.)*
Test	*Prueba (la) (n.)*
Testicles	*Testículos (los) (n.)*
Tetanus	*Tétano (el) (n.)*
Thermometer	*Termómetro (el) (n.)*

Thigh	*Muslo (el) (n.)*
Thin	*Delgado, a (adj.)*
Thorax	*Tórax (el) (n.)*
Thought	*Pensamiento (el) (n.)*
Throat	*Garganta (la) (n.)*
Thumb	*Pulgar (el) (n.)*
Thyroid	*Tiroides (la) (n.)*
Tie	*Amarrar (v.)*
Tightness	*Opresión (la) (n.)*
Tired	*Cansado, a (adj.)*
Tiredness	*Cansancio (el) (n.)*
Tissue	*Tejido (el) (n.)*
To crawl	*Gatear (v.)*
To get up	*Levantarse (v. r.)*
Tobacco	*Tabaco (el) (n.)*
Toe	*Dedo del pie (el) (n.)*
Toilet	*Escusado*
Tongue	*Lengua (la) (n.)*
Tonsil	*Amígdala (la) (n.)*
Tonsil	*Angina (la) (n.)*
Tonsillitis	*Amigdalitis (la) (n.)*
Tooth	*Diente (el) (n.)*
Toothpaste	*Pasta dentífrica (la) (n.)*
Tourniquet	*Ligadura (la) (n.)*
Toxic	*Tóxico, a (adj.)*
Toxins	*Toxinas (las) (n.)*
Trachea	*Tráquea (la) (n.)*
Training	*Entrenamiento (el) (n.)*
Tranquilizer	*Calmante (el) (n.)*
Transfusion	*Transfusión (la) (n.)*
Transmit	*Transmitir (v.)*
Transplant	*Transplante (el) (n.)*
Trauma	*Trauma (el) (n.)*
Treat	*Tratar (v.)*

Treatment	*Tratamiento (el) (n.)*
Tremors	*Temblor (el) (n.)*
Trouble	*Molestia (la) (n.)*
Tube	*Tubo (el) (n.)*
Tuberculin	*Tuberculina (la) (n.)*
Tuberculosis	*Tuberculosis (la) (n.)*
Tumor	*Tumor (el) (n.)*
Tweezers	*Pinza de cejas (la) (n.)*
Twins	*Mellizos (los) (n.) (adj.)*
Twist	*Torcedura (la) (n.)*
Ulcer	*Úlcera (la) (n.)*
Ultrasound	*Ultrasonido (el) (n.)*
Umbilical cord	*Cordón umbilical (el) (n.)*
Unbearable	*Insoportable (adj.)*
Under	*Debajo (adv.)*
Underwear	*Ropa interior (la) (n.)*
Undress	*Desvestir (v.)*
Uremia	*Uremia (la) (n.)*
Urethra	*Uretra (la) (n.)*
Uric	*Úrico, a (adj.)*
Uric acid	*Ácido úrico (el) (n.)*
Urinate	*Orinar (v.)*
Urine	*Orina (la) (n.)*
Urologist	*Urólogo (el-la) (n.)*
Uterus	*Útero (el) (n.)*
Uvula	*Campanilla (la) (n.)*
Uvula	*Úvula (la) (n.)*
Vaccine	*Vacuna (la) (n.)*
Vagina	*Vagina (la) (n.)*
Vaginitis	*Vaginitis (la) (n.)*
Vaginosis	*Vaginosis (la) (n.)*
Valve	*Válvula (la) (n.)*
Vaporizer	*Vaporizador (el) (n.)*
Varicose veins	*Várices (las) (n.)*

Vascular	*Vascular (adj.)*
Vasectomy	*Vasectomía (la) (n.)*
Vaseline	*Vaselina (la) (n.)*
Vein	*Vena (la) (n.)*
Venereal	*Venéreo, a (adj.)*
Vertebra	*Vértebra (la) (n.)*
Vertigo	*Vértigo (el) (n.)*
Violence	*Violencia (la) (n.)*
Virulent	*Virulento, a (adj.)*
Vision	*Visión (la) (n.)*
Visit	*Visita (la) (n.)*
Visual	*Visual (adj.)*
Vitamin	*Vitamina (la) (n.)*
Vomit	*Vomitar (v.)*
Waist	*Cintura (la) (n.)*
Wait	*Esperar (v.)*
Waiting room	*Sala de espera (la) (n.)*
Walk	*Caminar (v.)*
Ward	*Sala (la) (n.)*
Warning	*Advertencia (la) (n.)*
Wart	*Verruga (la) (n.)*
Wash	*Lavar (v.)*
Water	*Agua (el) (n.)*
Water bag	*Bolsa de agua (la) (n.)*
Weak	*Débil (adj.)*
Weakness	*Debilidad (la) (n.)*
Weigh	*Pesar (v.)*
Weight	*Peso (el) (n.)*
Well	*Bien (el) (n.) (adv.)*
Well being	*Bienestar (el) (n.)*
Wheelchair	*Silla de ruedas (la) (n.)*
Whooping cough	*Tosferina (la) (n.)*
Wife	*Esposa (la) (n.)*
Wine	*Vino (el) (n.)*

Wisdom tooth	*Muela del juicio (la) (n.)*
Woman	*Mujer (la) (n.)*
Womb	*Matriz (la) (n.)*
Worry	*Preocupación (la) (n.)*
Worst	*Peor (el) (n.)*
Wrist	*Muñeca (la) (n.)*
X-ray	*Radiografía (la) (n.)*
X-rays	*Rayos equis (los) (n.)*
Yeast	*Hongo (el) (n.)*
Yellowish	*Amarillento, a (adj.)*
Young girl	*Muchacha (la) (n.)*
Young man	*Muchacho (el) (n.)*
Zinc	*Zinc (el) (n.)*

Expresiones / Expressions

Español / Spanish

Inglés / English

COLOR

amarillo	*yellow*
azul	*blue*
blanco	*white*
café	*brown*
gris	*gray*
morado	*purple*
negro	*black*
rojo	*red*
rosa	*pink*
verde	*green*

EXPRESIONES DE TIEMPO

TIME EXPRESSIONS

A fines del mes	*At the end of the month*
A mediados de la semana	*In the middle of the week*
A principios del mes	*At the beginning of the month*
Amanecer	*Dawn*
Anochecer	*Dusk*
Ayer	*Yesterday*
Ayer por la tarde	*Yesterday afternoon*
El año entrante	*The coming year*
El año pasado	*Last year*
El próximo año	*Next year*
Fin de año	*End of the year*
Hace un año	*A year ago*
Hasta el martes	*Until Tuesday*
Hoy	*Today*
Madrugada	*Past midnight*
Mañana	*Tomorrow*

Mañana por la mañana	*Tomorrow morning*
Medianoche	*Midnight*
Mediodía	*Noon*
Noche	*Night*
Pasado mañana	*Day after tomorrow*
Tarde	*Afternoon*
Un momento	*One minute*

INSTRUCCIONES / INSTRUCTIONS

Abra la boca	*Open your mouth*
Acuéstese	*Lie down*
Ahorita vengo	*I'll be back*
Arriba	*Up*
Cierre el ojo derecho	*Close your right eye*
Coma bien	*Eat well*
Deje de tomar la medicina	*Stop taking the medication*
Despacio	*Slow*
Levántese	*Get up*
Mire mis dedos	*Look at my fingers*
No coma nada	*Don't eat anything*
No mueva la cabeza	*Don't move your head*
No se mueva	*Don't move*
No vomite	*Don't vomit*
Párese	*Stand*
Póngase de pie	*On your feet*
Póngase esta bata	*Put on this gown*
Quítese la ropa	*Take off your clothes*
Rápido	*Fast*
Regreso en un minuto	*I'll be back in a minute*
Repita por favor	*Repeat please*
Siéntese	*Sit*
Súbase aquí	*Step up here*
Tiene que quedarse en cama	*You must stay in bed*
Tome agua	*Drink water*

Tome jugos	*Drink juice*
Tome la medicina	*Take the medication*
Vomite	*Vomit*

PAÍSES

COUNTRIES

Argentina	*Argentina*
Bolivia	*Bolivia*
Chile	*Chile*
Colombia	*Colombia*
Costa Rica	*Costa Rica*
Cuba	*Cuba*
Ecuador	*Ecuador*
El Salvador	*El Salvador*
España	*España*
Guatemala	*Guatemala*
Honduras	*Honduras*
México	*Mexico*
Nicaragua	*Nicaragua*
Panamá	*Panamá*
Paraguay	*Paraguay*
Perú	*Peru*
Puerto Rico	*Puerto Rico*
Uruguay	*Uruguay*
Venezuela	*Venezuela*

CORTESÍA

COURTESY

¿Cómo?	*How?*
¿Cómo está?	*How are you?*
¿Mande?	*Excuse me?*
¿Me comprende?	*Do you understand?*
¿Me entiende?	*Do you understand?*
¿Qué?	*What?*
¿Qué dijo?	*What did you say?*
Adelante	*Come in*

Adiós	*Goodbye*
Buenas noches	*Good night*
Buenas tardes	*Good afternoon*
Buenos días	*Good morning*
Con permiso	*Excuse me*
Dígame	*Tell me*
Dispénseme	*I'm sorry*
Encantado	*Very glad*
Es un placer	*It's a pleasure*
Fue un placer	*It was a pleasure*
Hasta luego	*So long*
Hasta mañana	*Until tomorrow*
Le presento a Teresa	*May I introduce Teresa*
Muchas gracias	*Thank you*
Mucho gusto de conocerlo	*Very glad to meet you*
Muy amable	*Very kind*
Muy bien gracias	*Fine thank you*
Otra vez	*Again*
Pase	*Come in*
Perdón	*Pardon me*
Que le vaya bien	*Goodbye*
Yo soy el Doctor …	*I'm Doctor*
Yo soy José	*I'm Jose*

TIEMPO

TIME

año	*year*
día	*day*
hora	*hour*
mes	*month*
minuto	*minute*
segundo	*second*
semana	*week*
siglo	*century*

TÓXICO

ácido	*acid*
alcohol	*alcohol*
cloro	*bleach*
drogas	*drugs*
gasolina	*gasoline*
kerosene	*kerosene*
medicinas	*medications*
pintura	*paint*

TOXIC

NÚMERO

cero	*zero*
uno, una	*one*
dos	*two*
tres	*three*
cuatro	*four*
cinco	*five*
seis	*six*
siete	*seven*
ocho	*eight*
nueve	*nine*
diez	*ten*
once	*eleven*
doce	*twelve*
trece	*thirteen*
catorce	*fourteen*
quince	*fifteen*
dieciséis	*sixteen*
diecisiete	*seventeen*
dieciocho	*eighteen*
diecinueve	*nineteen*
veinte	*twenty*
treinta	*thirty*
cuarenta	*forty*

NUMBER

cincuenta	*fifty*
sesenta	*sixty*
setenta	*seventy*
ochenta	*eighty*
noventa	*ninety*
cien	*one hundred*
ciento uno	*one hundred and one*
doscientos	*two hundred*
trescientos	*three hundred*
quinientos	*five hundred*
mil	*one thousand*
dos mil	*two thousand*
tres mil	*three thousand*
un millón	*one million*

ORDINALES

ORDINALS

primero (a)	*first*
segundo (a)	*second*
tercero (a)	*third*
cuarto (a)	*fourth*
quinto (a)	*fifth*
sexto (a)	*sixth*
séptimo (a)	*seventh*
octavo (a)	*eighth*
noveno (a)	*ninth*
décimo (a)	*tenth*
undécimo (a)	*eleventh*
duodécimo (a)	*twelfth*
treceavo (a)	*thirteenth*
catorceavo (a)	*fourteenth*
quinceavo (a)	*fifteenth*
décimo sexto (a)	*sixteenth*
décimo séptimo (a)	*seventeenth*
décimo octavo (a)	*eighteenth*

décimo noveno (a)	*nineteenth*
vigésimo (a)	*twentieth*
trigésimo (a)	*thirtieth*

DÍAS DE LA SEMANA

DAYS OF THE WEEK

domingo	*Sunday*
lunes	*Monday*
martes	*Tuesday*
miércoles	*Wednesday*
jueves	*Thursday*
viernes	*Friday*
sábado	*Saturday*

MESES

MONTHS

enero	*January*
febrero	*February*
marzo	*March*
abril	*April*
mayo	*May*
junio	*June*
julio	*July*
agosto	*August*
septiembre	*September*
octubre	*October*
noviembre	*November*
diciembre	*December*